ANSWERS
(because we all have struggles)

Devotions for the Distressed
M. Meinert

© 2020 by Martha G. Meinert

All rights reserved. No portion of this book may be reproduced, stored in a retrieval system, or transmitted in any form or by any means—electronic, mechanical, photo copying, recording, scanning, or other—except for brief quotations in critical reviews or articles without the prior written permission of the publisher. For permission requests, write to the publisher at the address below.

M. Meinert Creations, LLC
4750 Vista View Ct.
Colorado Springs, CO 80915-1041

Scriptures taken from the Holy Bible, New International Version®, NIV®. Copyright © 1973, 1978, 1984, 2011 by Biblica, Inc.™ Used by permission of Zondervan. All rights reserved worldwide. www.zondervan.com

ISBN: 9781686401671

Dedications

This book of devotions is dedicated first to my faithful husband, Philip, who has stood by me through every crisis, a steady counterpoint to my roller coaster of emotions. I also wish to honor our son Tim and his wife, Cindy, for their constant Christian lives and love.

I write in memory of our son Ronald, who lived a brief eight years. At age seven he wrote, "When I grow up I want to be a mishinery because I would like teach people to learn about Jesus, and so they wonte pray to stachyous and now they like to learn about Jesus, and I would like to go to many countries."

He never had that opportunity, but because he lived and loved Jesus, it inspired me to write God's truths for others who struggle.

Author's Note

When I choose a book, I want to know about the author. Has this writer had experiences comparable to mine?

Life has presented many challenges. I had a dysfunctional childhood as an only child with an alcoholic father. By the time I was twenty, nine family members had died, including all my grandparents and my mother. Her death shocked my dad into sobriety. Later, he was able to help others addicted to alcohol.

I married at eighteen. Our first son, Ronald, was two when my Air Force husband, Phil, deployed to Vietnam. Tim was born when Ronald was four. Our family always attended church, but I had little understanding of God. When I was twenty-five, a friend asked me to study the Bible with her. It changed my life to learn God loved us so much that his son, Jesus, died on the cross for us despite our inability to live up to his standards. He came back to life with the promise we too can live eternally.

Ronald was killed in a wreck at age eight that also seriously injured Phil. Within a month, my aunt passed away and my father was diagnosed with a terminal illness. The love and support of many people plus Christian counseling helped me accept all the losses. In more recent years, my husband and I each have had several injuries and illnesses.

Some get upset with God and ask "Why?" when tragedy strikes. Others turn away from him. Scripture seldom answers why things happen. It teaches us how to live well, whatever our circumstances.

For years I have had the privilege of helping others through inspirational speaking, and I formerly facilitated a grief support program. I tell everyone, "Read God's instruction book before all else fails!"

This devotion book is for those who are distressed. It shares God's truths and encourages us to pray according to the Lord's simple pattern, paraphrased at the bottom of each devotion.

To God be all praise and thanksgiving.

Marty

Martha ("Marty") Lewis Meinert

Table of Contents

Chapter 1. 1

Chapter 2. 17

Chapter 3. 33

Chapter 4. 49

Chapter 5. 65

Chapter 6. 81

Chapter 7. 97

Chapter 8. 113

Chapter 9. 129

Chapter 10. 145

Chapter 11. 161

Chapter 12. 177

Pain is Pain: A Poem by M. Meinert 193

Acknowledgments 195

Chapter 1

A Set Menu 2

Be Still 3

Cling to Faith 4

Elasticity 5

For the Distressed... 6

Hurt Feelings 7

Life for "Smarties" 8

Mental Round-up 9

Parable of Popcorn 10

Reach Out for Relief 11

Seeing or Believing 12

Telling the Truth 13

Trapped 14

What Now? 15

A Set Menu

Living a Christian life is not an invitation to "salad bar spirituality." It is not ours to pick and choose what we believe and obey. Life will be much better if we follow God's instructions. He designed them for our well-being.

Deuteronomy 11:26-28
[26] See, I am setting before you today a blessing and a curse—[27] the blessing if you obey the commands of the Lord your God that I am giving you today; [28] the curse if you disobey the commands of the Lord your God and turn from the way that I command you today by following other gods, which you have not known.

Prayer Guide
Our holy, heavenly Father, may your will prevail. Supply our daily needs. Forgive our sins as we forgive others. Protect us from temptation and rescue us from evil. We pray through the name, power and blood of our Lord, Jesus. Amen.

Be Still

An eye exercise to help restore balance calls for the patient to rotate his head from side to side while keeping his eyes focused on one spot about eight feet away. This is difficult to do while maintaining narrow focus. This exercise serves as a good analogy for trying to focus on God and his instructions in the Bible. It is so hard to focus unless we become still. If we are moving all about and distracted by activities and extraneous motion, we cannot focus clearly on God. Life's distractions tempt us to look elsewhere, but the only answer is to look to our Lord and his instructions. If we are not concentrating on God, we will see all the false teachings of men.

Psalm 46:10
[10] He says, "Be still, and know that I am God;
 I will be exalted among the nations,
 I will be exalted in the earth."

Hebrews 12:2-3
[2] fixing our eyes on Jesus, the pioneer and perfecter of faith. For the joy set before him he endured the cross, scorning its shame, and sat down at the right hand of the throne of God. [3] Consider him who endured such opposition from sinners, so that you will not grow weary and lose heart.

Prayer Guide
Our holy, heavenly Father, may your will prevail. Supply our daily needs. Forgive our sins as we forgive others. Protect us from temptation and rescue us from evil. We pray through the name, power and blood of our Lord, Jesus. Amen.

Cling to Faith

Whether our moods are up, down or sideways, we must cling to faith in God as fact. Emotions are not dependable, but God is constant and consistent. Faith is a choice and makes all the difference.

2 Chronicles 20:20
[20] Early in the morning they left for the Desert of Tekoa. As they set out, Jehoshaphat stood and said, "Listen to me, Judah and people of Jerusalem! Have faith in the Lord your God and you will be upheld; have faith in his prophets and you will be successful."

Isaiah 7:9b
[9b] "If you do not stand firm in your faith,
 you will not stand at all.'"

Hebrews 11:1,3,6
[1] Now faith is confidence in what we hope for and assurance about what we do not see.

[3] By faith we understand that the universe was formed at God's command, so that what is seen was not made out of what was visible.

[6] And without faith it is impossible to please God, because anyone who comes to him must believe that he exists and that he rewards those who earnestly seek him.

2 Corinthians 5:7
[7] For we live by faith, not by sight.

Prayer Guide
Our holy, heavenly Father, may your will prevail. Supply our daily needs. Forgive our sins as we forgive others. Protect us from temptation and rescue us from evil. We pray through the name, power and blood of our Lord, Jesus. Amen.

Elasticity

Sometimes obligations, irritations and responsibilities stretch us to the breaking point. What can we do when our own capabilities are inadequate, when the rubber bands holding our lives together are about to snap? We seek strength and flexibility beyond our own limits. We cannot stand one more assault, so we turn to God, whose abilities are unlimited.

Psalm 55:16-18

16 As for me, I call to God,
    and the LORD saves me.
17 Evening, morning and noon
    I cry out in distress,
    and he hears my voice.
18 He rescues me unharmed
    from the battle waged against me,
    even though many oppose me.

Psalm 62:1-2

1 Truly my soul finds rest in God;
    my salvation comes from him.
2 Truly he is my rock and my salvation;
    he is my fortress, I will never be shaken.

Prayer Guide
Our holy, heavenly Father, may your will prevail. Supply our daily needs. Forgive our sins as we forgive others. Protect us from temptation and rescue us from evil. We pray through the name, power and blood of our Lord, Jesus. Amen.

For the Distressed...

Many of us get upset with God when tragedy strikes, whether it is our own personal loss or that of others. We want to ask "Why?" Sometimes we become so angry with God that we turn away from him. Scripture never suggests that we will understand the reasons behind the events of our lives. We are probably asking the wrong question when we cry out "Why?" The better question is "How?" How can we make it through this time? The Bible says God will never leave us alone. We have been given the Holy Spirit, and he will provide what we truly need.

Deuteronomy 29:29
[29] The secret things belong to the Lord our God, but the things revealed belong to us and to our children forever, that we may follow all the words of this law.

John 15:26-27
[26] "When the Advocate comes, whom I will send to you from the Father—the Spirit of truth who goes out from the Father—he will testify about me. [27] And you also must testify, for you have been with me from the beginning."

John 16:22
[22] So with you: Now is your time of grief, but I will see you again and you will rejoice, and no one will take away your joy.

Prayer Guide
Our holy, heavenly Father, may your will prevail. Supply our daily needs. Forgive our sins as we forgive others. Protect us from temptation and rescue us from evil. We pray through the name, power and blood of our Lord, Jesus. Amen.

Hurt Feelings

Most of the time when others hurt us, the hurt is compounded because those individuals are persons important in our lives. We don't notice so much when other people make comments because they are not as significant in our lives. We need to assess whether other's words are true and if there is sufficient reason for us to change. We can seldom change others and truly are responsible only for our own behavior and speech. If we have offended another, should we be asking that person for forgiveness before we come to the Lord with offerings? If someone has offended us, is it something that needs to be discussed, and what is the Godly way to do so?

Matthew 5:23-24
[23] "Therefore, if you are offering your gift at the altar and there remember that your brother or sister has something against you,
[24] leave your gift there in front of the altar. First go and be reconciled to them; then come and offer your gift."

Matthew 18:15
[15] "If your brother or sister sins, go and point out their fault, just between the two of you. If they listen to you, you have won them over."

Prayer Guide
Our holy, heavenly Father, may your will prevail. Supply our daily needs. Forgive our sins as we forgive others. Protect us from temptation and rescue us from evil. We pray through the name, power and blood of our Lord, Jesus. Amen.

Life for "Smarties"

There is a whole series of simple instruction books on many subjects for "Dummies." It'd be nice, but life itself cannot be reduced to following a set of rules that always work out if one just puts the pieces together correctly. Rather, the Bible provides truths and guidelines for those smart enough and humble enough to apply the wisdom readily available. Jesus himself reduced it to two principles: (1) love God with everything you've got, and (2) love others as yourselves. (Easy to say, sometimes much harder to carry out!)

Deuteronomy 4:39-40
[39] Acknowledge and take to heart this day that the LORD is God in heaven above and on the earth below. There is no other. [40] Keep his decrees and commands, which I am giving you today, so that it may go well with you and your children after you and that you may live long in the land the LORD your God gives you for all time.

Mark 12:30-31
[30] "'Love the Lord your God with all your heart and with all your soul and with all your mind and with all your strength.' [31] The second is this: 'Love your neighbor as yourself.' There is no commandment greater than these."

Prayer Guide
Our holy, heavenly Father, may your will prevail. Supply our daily needs. Forgive our sins as we forgive others. Protect us from temptation and rescue us from evil. We pray through the name, power and blood of our Lord, Jesus. Amen.

Mental Round-up

When stray thoughts and fears crowd our minds and push away the confidence and comfort of the Lord, we must round them up, lassoing them like wandering livestock to bring them into the corral. Then we can turn them over to God for him to deal with according to his plan. We need to give him all the fears, the "what ifs" and even the "what is" of overwhelming circumstances. Our heavenly Father, our Lord Jesus and the mighty Holy Spirit can deal with the negative thoughts that plague us. We relinquish them to divine disposal.

Romans 8:15
[15] The Spirit you received does not make you slaves, so that you live in fear again; rather, the Spirit you received brought about your adoption to sonship. And by him we cry, "*Abba*, Father."

2 Corinthians 10:4-5
[4] The weapons we fight with are not the weapons of the world. On the contrary, they have divine power to demolish strongholds. [5] We demolish arguments and every pretension that sets itself up against the knowledge of God, and we take captive every thought to make it obedient to Christ.

1 John 4:18
[18] There is no fear in love. But perfect love drives out fear, because fear has to do with punishment. The one who fears is not made perfect in love.

Prayer Guide
Our holy, heavenly Father, may your will prevail. Supply our daily needs. Forgive our sins as we forgive others. Protect us from temptation and rescue us from evil. We pray through the name, power and blood of our Lord, Jesus. Amen.

Parable of Popcorn

Popcorn is inedible unless the kernels are heated to the point of nearly burning. Then, each little kernel bursts into a blossom of tastiness. We often require the heat of adversity to transform us into usefulness. Then we can nurture others with what we have learned through surviving the fire.

1 Corinthians 3:12-15

[12] If anyone builds on this foundation using gold, silver, costly stones, wood, hay or straw, [13] their work will be shown for what it is, because the Day will bring it to light. It will be revealed with fire, and the fire will test the quality of each person's work. [14] If what has been built survives, the builder will receive a reward. [15] If it is burned up, the builder will suffer loss but yet will be saved—even though only as one escaping through the flames.

Prayer Guide

Our holy, heavenly Father, may your will prevail. Supply our daily needs. Forgive our sins as we forgive others. Protect us from temptation and rescue us from evil. We pray through the name, power and blood of our Lord, Jesus. Amen.

Reach Out for Relief

Whether single or married, an only child or part of a large family, we all feel lonely at times. The best way to alleviate loneliness is to reach out to another soul who may be hurting. It is not hard to find people in need of a kind word or a friendly touch. It does require looking at and paying attention to others. If none of your peers has such a problem, go visit an elderly person or volunteer to read to children in grade school. Remember too that the Lord is your ultimate friend.

Colossians 3:15-16
[15] Let the peace of Christ rule in your hearts, since as members of one body you were called to peace. And be thankful. [16] Let the message of Christ dwell among you richly as you teach and admonish one another with all wisdom through psalms, hymns, and songs from the Spirit, singing to God with gratitude in your hearts.

Hebrews 3:13
[13] But encourage one another daily, as long as it is called "Today," so that none of you may be hardened by sin's deceitfulness.

Hebrews 4:16
[16] Let us then approach God's throne of grace with confidence, so that we may receive mercy and find grace to help us in our time of need.

Prayer Guide
Our holy, heavenly Father, may your will prevail. Supply our daily needs. Forgive our sins as we forgive others. Protect us from temptation and rescue us from evil. We pray through the name, power and blood of our Lord, Jesus. Amen.

Seeing or Believing?

We all know and understand the phrase "seeing is believing." But do we really understand that believing is also seeing? When we believe, we see an oak tree in an acorn, a whole stalk of corn in a kernel and a row of flowers in a packet of seeds. We even see LIFE beyond a tombstone or an urn of ashes when we believe in the creator of life.

John 20:27-29
[27] Then he said to Thomas, "Put your finger here; see my hands. Reach out your hand and put it into my side. Stop doubting and believe."
[28] Thomas said to him, "My Lord and my God!"
[29] Then Jesus told him, "Because you have seen me, you have believed; blessed are those who have not seen and yet have believed."

Acts 2:36-39
[36] "Therefore let all Israel be assured of this: God has made this Jesus, whom you crucified, both Lord and Messiah."
[37] When the people heard this, they were cut to the heart and said to Peter and the other apostles, "Brothers, what shall we do?"
[38] Peter replied, "Repent and be baptized, every one of you, in the name of Jesus Christ for the forgiveness of your sins. And you will receive the gift of the Holy Spirit. [39] The promise is for you and your children and for all who are far off—for all whom the Lord our God will call."

Prayer Guide
Our holy, heavenly Father, may your will prevail. Supply our daily needs. Forgive our sins as we forgive others. Protect us from temptation and rescue us from evil. We pray through the name, power and blood of our Lord, Jesus. Amen.

Telling the Truth

My mother said the grace of "tact" was the art of telling the truth without hurting people's feelings. Sometimes that is very difficult. There can be a fine line between speaking the truth with compassion and telling a "little white lie." We are responsible for our own attitudes, actions and words. Sometimes the truth does hurt. Sometimes silence is a lie. When we do decide to correct or speak difficult words to others, let's attempt to do so with kindness.

Ephesians 4:15,25,29

[15] Instead, speaking the truth in love, we will grow to become in every respect the mature body of him who is the head, that is, Christ.

[25] Therefore each of you must put off falsehood and speak truthfully to your neighbor, for we are all members of one body.

[29] Do not let any unwholesome talk come out of your mouths, but only what is helpful for building others up according to their needs, that it may benefit those who listen.

Prayer Guide
Our holy, heavenly Father, may your will prevail. Supply our daily needs. Forgive our sins as we forgive others. Protect us from temptation and rescue us from evil. We pray through the name, power and blood of our Lord, Jesus. Amen.

Trapped

When we are feeling trapped, our only thought is of escape. If we have pain, we want relief; if we have loss, we want restitution; if we are in conflict, we seek peace. When we desire, we crave fulfillment. We are restless people; we want what was or we want what is not yet to be. Relentlessly we pursue gratification. The answer is not escape from the circumstance, it is learning to live within what is.

Isaiah 26:3
[3] You will keep in perfect peace
those whose minds are steadfast,
because they trust in you.

Philippians 4:12
[12] I know what it is to be in need, and I know what it is to have plenty. I have learned the secret of being content in any and every situation, whether well fed or hungry, whether living in plenty or in want.

2 Peter 1:3-4
[3] His divine power has given us everything we need for a godly life through our knowledge of him who called us by his own glory and goodness. [4] Through these he has given us his very great and precious promises, so that through them you may participate in the divine nature, having escaped the corruption in the world caused by evil desires.

Prayer Guide
Our holy, heavenly Father, may your will prevail. Supply our daily needs. Forgive our sins as we forgive others. Protect us from temptation and rescue us from evil. We pray through the name, power and blood of our Lord, Jesus. Amen.

What Now?

How do we keep on keeping on when God seems silent or when he answers "Wait" or even "No" to our urgent pleas? It is a conscious decision to trust the Lord regardless of the outcome.

Psalm 50:15
[15] "and call on me in the day of trouble;
   I will deliver you, and you will honor me."

John 6:68
[68] Simon Peter answered him, "Lord, to whom shall we go? You have the words of eternal life."

John 16:33
[33] "I have told you these things, so that in me you may have peace. In this world you will have trouble. But take heart! I have overcome the world."

Prayer Guide
Our holy, heavenly Father, may your will prevail. Supply our daily needs. Forgive our sins as we forgive others. Protect us from temptation and rescue us from evil. We pray through the name, power and blood of our Lord, Jesus. Amen.

Chapter 2

A Smooth Flight, or Not 18

Being Prepared 19

Clouds 20

Divine Guidance 21

Endurance 22

Forgive Anyway 23

Illumination 24

Mirror, Mirror 25

Particulars or Principles? 26

Reaction or Reality 27

Seeing the Invisible 28

Temptation Tapping 29

True Trust 30

Worthiness 31

A Smooth Flight, or Not

We want our lives to run smoothly—having enough money, peace in the family, decent health, fill in the blank. If our flight through life has been smooth thus far, we can be grateful. But continue to be grateful when turbulence is encountered. None of us make our entire journey without a few rough bumps. This doesn't mean our plane is crashing.

Psalm 31:14-15
[14] But I trust in you, LORD;
    I say, "You are my God."
[15] My times are in your hands;
    deliver me from the hands of my enemies,
    from those who pursue me.

Philippians 1:6
[6] being confident of this, that he who began a good work in you will carry it on to completion until the day of Christ Jesus.

James 1:12
[12] Blessed is the one who perseveres under trial because, having stood the test, that person will receive the crown of life that the Lord has promised to those who love him.

Prayer Guide
Our holy, heavenly Father, may your will prevail. Supply our daily needs. Forgive our sins as we forgive others. Protect us from temptation and rescue us from evil. We pray through the name, power and blood of our Lord, Jesus. Amen.

Being Prepared

The Boy Scout motto, "Be prepared," was first used in England in 1907 by the founder, Robert Baden-Powell. It means we always should be aware of situations and educate ourselves on the basics of how to handle most anything. That does not mean we should be constantly asking "But what if..." in order to be prepared for absolutely every possible scenario, which would be overwhelming. Most of the things we worry about do not happen. For the small percentage of adversities that do strike us, the most important thing is knowing what the Bible teaches about such instances and using common sense. The late American president Teddy Roosevelt said, "Walk softly, but carry a big stick." He was speaking politically about the stance of nations. In our personal lives, it could mean being practical and not hiking in the forest without some protection and preparation, such as a walking stick, a compass and a trail map. It is not suggesting we carry a big rifle (unless we live in grizzly bear country). In any situation, learning the principles of God's word will prepare us better than any sort of weapon or philosophy.

Proverbs 16:20
[20] Whoever gives heed to instruction prospers,
  and blessed is the one who trusts in the LORD.

Matthew 10:16
[16] "I am sending you out like sheep among wolves. Therefore be as shrewd as snakes and as innocent as doves."

1 Peter 5:6-7
[6] Humble yourselves, therefore, under God's mighty hand, that he may lift you up in due time. [7] Cast all your anxiety on him because he cares for you.

Prayer Guide
Our holy, heavenly Father, may your will prevail. Supply our daily needs. Forgive our sins as we forgive others. Protect us from temptation and rescue us from evil. We pray through the name, power and blood of our Lord, Jesus. Amen.

Clouds

Flying through the clouds gives us a different perspective that we can apply to our life's situations. If the weather is clear when we reach altitude (and we have a window seat), we can view the earth below with a much wider view than when we're traveling along the ground. We can see much farther and detect possible obstacles that we can't see from a car or on foot. However, if there is low cloud cover, the weather appears gloomy, dark and threatening from the ground. But if we're flying, once we ascend through the clouds, we are met with brilliant sunshine and cannot see what we have left behind. There are times when we fly that the clouds are so thick our whole trip is closed in. We are oppressed by not being able to see where we came from or where we are headed. This is when we trust the pilots the most. We are helpless and must have faith that those who know the plane and how it works can get us safely to our destination. (The very same thing is true when the way is clear, we simply don't think about it as much when we can see where we are headed.) Therefore, whether our spiritual sky is clear or cloudy, we must trust God as our pilot who always knows the best way to fly.

Exodus 13:21a
[21a] By day the Lord went ahead of them in a pillar of cloud to guide them on their way...

Psalm 119:105
[105] Your word is a lamp for my feet,
a light on my path.

Hebrews 12:2
[2] fixing our eyes on Jesus, the pioneer and perfecter of faith. For the joy set before him he endured the cross, scorning its shame, and sat down at the right hand of the throne of God.

Prayer Guide
Our holy, heavenly Father, may your will prevail. Supply our daily needs. Forgive our sins as we forgive others. Protect us from temptation and rescue us from evil. We pray through the name, power and blood of our Lord, Jesus. Amen.

Divine Guidance

Because God's word, the Bible, is living, it can speak to us from early childhood to old age. Little children can learn the great stories, such as the story of faithful Noah and his family being saved on the ark through the great flood. Older folks can find comfort and peace through the promises of the Lord that we will never be alone.

Joshua 1:9
9 "Have I not commanded you? Be strong and courageous. Do not be afraid; do not be discouraged, for the Lord your God will be with you wherever you go."

Psalm 119:130
130   The unfolding of your words gives light;
       it gives understanding to the simple.

Hebrews 4:12
12 For the word of God is alive and active. Sharper than any double-edged sword, it penetrates even to dividing soul and spirit, joints and marrow; it judges the thoughts and attitudes of the heart.

Prayer Guide
Our holy, heavenly Father, may your will prevail. Supply our daily needs. Forgive our sins as we forgive others. Protect us from temptation and rescue us from evil. We pray through the name, power and blood of our Lord, Jesus. Amen.

Endurance

When we experience distress, it is pretty natural to feel like no one else has traveled this same rough road. Yet the truth is that while my exact experience may be unique, difficulty is common to every person. It is the human condition to endure struggles because we are living in a fallen world. Remember that to stress a muscle is to strengthen it. So it also is with one's soul.

2 Corinthians 1:6-7
[6] If we are distressed, it is for your comfort and salvation; if we are comforted, it is for your comfort, which produces in you patient endurance of the same sufferings we suffer. [7] And our hope for you is firm, because we know that just as you share in our sufferings, so also you share in our comfort.

James 1:4
[4] Let perseverance finish its work so that you may be mature and complete, not lacking anything.

1 Peter 1:7
[7] These have come so that the proven genuineness of your faith—of greater worth than gold, which perishes even though refined by fire—may result in praise, glory and honor when Jesus Christ is revealed.

Prayer Guide
Our holy, heavenly Father, may your will prevail. Supply our daily needs. Forgive our sins as we forgive others. Protect us from temptation and rescue us from evil. We pray through the name, power and blood of our Lord, Jesus. Amen.

Forgive Anyway

Of all the lessons we need to learn, forgiveness is one of the most difficult. When we have been hurt, we want the offender to be sorry. The worse the sin against us, usually the more we want the person to be punished. God promises justice in the end, but we are taught through Scripture to forgive now. Forgiving is not saying the action against us was OK. Forgiveness is God's way of saying "I choose to set the guilty free." For us it is a conscious decision and often a lengthy process, not based on emotion but done in obedience to God's teachings and often only accomplished with prayer and help from the Holy Spirit. At times we have to ask for help even to decide to forgive.

Matthew 5:44-45
[44] But I tell you, love your enemies and pray for those who persecute you, [45] that you may be children of your Father in heaven. He causes his sun to rise on the evil and the good, and sends rain on the righteous and the unrighteous.

Matthew 18:21-22
[21] Then Peter came to Jesus and asked, "Lord, how many times shall I forgive my brother or sister who sins against me? Up to seven times?" [22] Jesus answered, "I tell you, not seven times, but seventy-seven times."

Luke 6:35-36
[35] But love your enemies, do good to them, and lend to them without expecting to get anything back. Then your reward will be great, and you will be children of the Most High, because he is kind to the ungrateful and wicked. [36] Be merciful, just as your Father is merciful.

Prayer Guide
Our holy, heavenly Father, may your will prevail. Supply our daily needs. Forgive our sins as we forgive others. Protect us from temptation and rescue us from evil. We pray through the name, power and blood of our Lord, Jesus. Amen.

Illumination

The human eye cannot perceive color in dim light, nor can it focus clearly without much light. Yet just a little light is enough to see so we can safely navigate the darkness—as long as we keep our eyes on that light and walk slowly and carefully. Darkness cannot spread and overwhelm light. If you want to see and understand life, look to Jesus, who is the source of light.

Psalm 112:4
[4] Even in darkness light dawns for the upright,
for those who are gracious and compassionate and righteous.

Matthew 5:14-16
[14] "You are the light of the world. A town built on a hill cannot be hidden. [15] Neither do people light a lamp and put it under a bowl. Instead they put it on its stand, and it gives light to everyone in the house. [16] In the same way, let your light shine before others, that they may see your good deeds and glorify your Father in heaven."

Luke 8:16
[16] "No one lights a lamp and hides it in a clay jar or puts it under a bed. Instead, they put it on a stand, so that those who come in can see the light."

John 1:4-5
[4] In him was life, and that life was the light of all mankind. [5] The light shines in the darkness, and the darkness has not overcome it.

Prayer Guide
Our holy, heavenly Father, may your will prevail. Supply our daily needs. Forgive our sins as we forgive others. Protect us from temptation and rescue us from evil. We pray through the name, power and blood of our Lord, Jesus. Amen.

Mirror, Mirror...

Whether we answer the old question "Who's the fairest?" with a "Yes, me" or "No way, never me," we have an out-of-focus view. Instead of looking in the mirror with flawed judgment every day, we need to look to God for an accurate assessment of ourselves. The most beautiful or handsome is subject to times of decay or unforeseen events. A better emphasis would be checking our internal qualities. In God's view we are beloved; we are part of his family. We find our true identity and beauty in Christ.

1 Samuel 16:7
[7] But the Lord said to Samuel, "Do not consider his appearance or his height, for I have rejected him. The Lord does not look at the things people look at. People look at the outward appearance, but the Lord looks at the heart."

Romans 12:2
[2] Do not conform to the pattern of this world, but be transformed by the renewing of your mind. Then you will be able to test and approve what God's will is—his good, pleasing and perfect will.

2 Corinthians 4:16,18
[16] Therefore we do not lose heart. Though outwardly we are wasting away, yet inwardly we are being renewed day by day.

[18] So we fix our eyes not on what is seen, but on what is unseen, since what is seen is temporary, but what is unseen is eternal.

1 John 3:1
[1] See what great love the Father has lavished on us, that we should be called children of God! And that is what we are! The reason the world does not know us is that it did not know him.

Prayer Guide
Our holy, heavenly Father, may your will prevail. Supply our daily needs. Forgive our sins as we forgive others. Protect us from temptation and rescue us from evil. We pray through the name, power and blood of our Lord, Jesus. Amen.

Particulars or Principles?

Many find it easier to keep a list of rules than to live according to principles. The religious leaders of Jesus' day were called Pharisees and had memorized the details of the laws and judged others, often harshly, by how well they adhered to them. Jesus taught the principle of loving God first and foremost and all others next. If we truly live by love, then obeying God's ways will follow. Jesus Christ taught us our motives matter the most.

Matthew 6:1-4
[1] "Be careful not to practice your righteousness in front of others to be seen by them. If you do, you will have no reward from your Father in heaven.

[2] "So when you give to the needy, do not announce it with trumpets, as the hypocrites do in the synagogues and on the streets, to be honored by others. Truly I tell you, they have received their reward in full. [3] But when you give to the needy, do not let your left hand know what your right hand is doing, [4] so that your giving may be in secret. Then your Father, who sees what is done in secret, will reward you."

Luke 11:42
[42] "Woe to you Pharisees, because you give God a tenth of your mint, rue and all other kinds of garden herbs, but you neglect justice and the love of God. You should have practiced the latter without leaving the former undone.

John 13:34
[34] "A new command I give you: Love one another. As I have loved you, so you must love one another."

Prayer Guide
Our holy, heavenly Father, may your will prevail. Supply our daily needs. Forgive our sins as we forgive others. Protect us from temptation and rescue us from evil. We pray through the name, power and blood of our Lord, Jesus. Amen.

Reaction or Reality

Instant emotional reactions do not equal reality. A counselor's good advice said, if "A" is the circumstance, such as a loved one being very late arriving when he promised, and "C" could be a terrible accident, do not skip over "B," which can be all sorts of other realities. There may have been a traffic jam, a meeting going long, a flat tire or all sorts of alternative situations. In the rare instance of actual tragedy, we can gain God's strength to deal with it. For the other 99% of the time, we can train ourselves to breathe deeply and change our default panic mode to thought-out and prayed-about responses.

Psalm 120:1
[1] I call on the Lord in my distress,
and he answers me.

2 Timothy 1:7
[7] For the Spirit God gave us does not make us timid, but gives us power, love and self-discipline.

1 John 4:18
[18] There is no fear in love. But perfect love drives out fear, because fear has to do with punishment. The one who fears is not made perfect in love.

Prayer Guide
Our holy, heavenly Father, may your will prevail. Supply our daily needs. Forgive our sins as we forgive others. Protect us from temptation and rescue us from evil. We pray through the name, power and blood of our Lord, Jesus. Amen.

Seeing the Invisible

With trouble at every turn, we must learn to "see" the invisible things of God. There is a continual battle being waged between good and evil, we just fail to recognize it. The good news is on the side of the Christian in this spiritual war. God wants everything that is best for us—whether that's lessons learned through difficulty or praises of joy over answered prayers.

Psalm 138:7
[7] Though I walk in the midst of trouble,
    you preserve my life.
You stretch out your hand against the anger of my foes;
    with your right hand you save me.

Romans 8:25-27
[25] But if we hope for what we do not yet have, we wait for it patiently. [26] In the same way, the Spirit helps us in our weakness. We do not know what we ought to pray for, but the Spirit himself intercedes for us through wordless groans. [27] And he who searches our hearts knows the mind of the Spirit, because the Spirit intercedes for God's people in accordance with the will of God.

[37] No, in all these things we are more than conquerors through him who loved us. [38] For I am convinced that neither death nor life, neither angels nor demons, neither the present nor the future, nor any powers, [39] neither height nor depth, nor anything else in all creation, will be able to separate us from the love of God that is in Christ Jesus our Lord.

Prayer Guide
Our holy, heavenly Father, may your will prevail. Supply our daily needs. Forgive our sins as we forgive others. Protect us from temptation and rescue us from evil. We pray through the name, power and blood of our Lord, Jesus. Amen.

Temptation Tapping

Temptation may not burst through your door, but it will, at some point, come tap on your windows! Whether it is in the form of giving in to addictions, adultery, or even envy or inappropriate anger, it will seek you out. It is in the devil's department of operations. How then shall we respond? We follow Jesus' example when he was tempted by the devil during forty days in the desert. We answer with resistance, prayer and the power of God's word.

Luke 4:12-13
[12] Jesus answered, "It is said: 'Do not put the Lord your God to the test.'"
[13] When the devil had finished all this tempting, he left him until an opportune time.

James 1:13-14
[13] When tempted, no one should say, "God is tempting me." For God cannot be tempted by evil, nor does he tempt anyone; [14] but each person is tempted when they are dragged away by their own evil desire and enticed.

James 4:7-8,13-15
[7] Submit yourselves, then, to God. Resist the devil, and he will flee from you. [8] Come near to God and he will come near to you. Wash your hands, you sinners, and purify your hearts, you double-minded.

[13] Now listen, you who say, "Today or tomorrow we will go to this or that city, spend a year there, carry on business and make money." [14] Why, you do not even know what will happen tomorrow. What is your life? You are a mist that appears for a little while and then vanishes. [15] Instead, you ought to say, "If it is the Lord's will, we will live and do this or that."

Prayer Guide

Our holy, heavenly Father, may your will prevail. Supply our daily needs. Forgive our sins as we forgive others. Protect us from temptation and rescue us from evil. We pray through the name, power and blood of our Lord, Jesus. Amen.

True Trust

Those of us who have suffered discord, setbacks and tragedies have issues with trust. Because something bad happened in our past, we fear it will happen again in our future. We must learn to trust that God is consistently good whether our lives are hard or pleasant. Usually life is a mix of both. True trust believes that a good God will help us through the tough times and bless us in all situations.

Psalm 31:19

19 How abundant are the good things
    that you have stored up for those who fear you,
  that you bestow in the sight of all,
    on those who take refuge in you.

Psalm 107:4-6

4   wandered in desert wastelands,
      finding no way to a city where they could settle.
5   They were hungry and thirsty,
      and their lives ebbed away.
6   Then they cried out to the LORD in their trouble,
      and he delivered them from their distress.

Prayer Guide
Our holy, heavenly Father, may your will prevail. Supply our daily needs. Forgive our sins as we forgive others. Protect us from temptation and rescue us from evil. We pray through the name, power and blood of our Lord, Jesus. Amen.

Worthiness

It isn't what we "do" that is nearly as important as how we love God and others. Sometimes love is shown through hard work and sometimes it's shown through kind words and deeds, but it is often accompanied by prayer. Our culture says we are not worth much if we clean toilets for a living. Not true! If we were the CEO of a Fortune 500 company but showed no love and respect toward others, we would not be worthy. We would be a failure in life's most important aspect.

1 Corinthians 13:4
[4] Love is patient, love is kind. It does not envy, it does not boast, it is not proud.

Colossians 3:23-24
[23] Whatever you do, work at it with all your heart, as working for the Lord, not for human masters, [24] since you know that you will receive an inheritance from the Lord as a reward. It is the Lord Christ you are serving.

Prayer Guide

Our holy, heavenly Father, may your will prevail. Supply our daily needs. Forgive our sins as we forgive others. Protect us from temptation and rescue us from evil. We pray through the name, power and blood of our Lord, Jesus. Amen.

Chapter 3

About Rainbows 34

Blinding Storms 35

Conquering Mountains 36

Enough? 37

Forgiveness. 38

Impossible Requirements 39

Listen Up 40

Mental Mud 41

Peace 42

Read and Heed 43

Seeking Success 44

Tending to Disorder 45

Trust or Fear? 46

Where Is My Help? 47

About Rainbows

The phenomena of rainbows are visible, thanks to light shining through rain against a backdrop of dark clouds. You cannot fully experience this aspect of God's created beauty without the dark elements. Our lives exhibit a parallel quality: The brightest, loveliest "colors" (memories or experiences) show up best contrasted with life's darker, more difficult moments. An interesting fact about rainbows is that viewed from high altitude, such as through an airplane window, they can appear as perfect circles of concentric bands of colors. A rainbow is more than a symbol of God's forgiveness and promise not to destroy the world again by flood. It represents eternity as a circle that has no beginning or end. When from the earth we see only a half circle, it is because we are not in a position to view the whole picture.

Genesis 9:13-16
[13] "I have set my rainbow in the clouds, and it will be the sign of the covenant between me and the earth. [14] Whenever I bring clouds over the earth and the rainbow appears in the clouds, [15] I will remember my covenant between me and you and all living creatures of every kind. Never again will the waters become a flood to destroy all life. [16] Whenever the rainbow appears in the clouds, I will see it and remember the everlasting covenant between God and all living creatures of every kind on the earth."

Revelation 4:2-3
[2] At once I was in the Spirit, and there before me was a throne in heaven with someone sitting on it. [3] And the one who sat there had the appearance of jasper and ruby. A rainbow that shone like an emerald encircled the throne.

Prayer Guide
Our holy, heavenly Father, may your will prevail. Supply our daily needs. Forgive our sins as we forgive others. Protect us from temptation and rescue us from evil. We pray through the name, power and blood of our Lord, Jesus. Amen.

Blinding Storms

Life can be a blizzard, blowing about us, snow coming from every direction until we can no longer see the way. Whether it is trouble, loss or illness, our storm can be blinding. We want to get out of it, to be able to see something familiar. When the storm starts to abate, we begin to glimpse a source of light. Yet we must not be deceived; the wind can change direction and once more we are closed in. God will guide us through a blizzard or shelter us from the storm.

Psalm 46:1
1   God is our refuge and strength,
        an ever-present help in trouble.

Psalm 27:5,14
5   For in the day of trouble
        he will keep me safe in his dwelling;
     he will hide me in the shelter of his sacred tent
        and set me high upon a rock.

14   Wait for the LORD;
        be strong and take heart
     and wait for the LORD.

Isaiah 41:10
10   So do not fear, for I am with you;
        do not be dismayed, for I am your God.
     I will strengthen you and help you;
        I will uphold you with my righteous right hand.

Prayer Guide
Our holy, heavenly Father, may your will prevail. Supply our daily needs. Forgive our sins as we forgive others. Protect us from temptation and rescue us from evil. We pray through the name, power and blood of our Lord, Jesus. Amen.

Conquering Mountains

Earlier generations often had clichés for every occasion. One I heard regularly repeated when I was being an overly dramatic teen was "Don't make mountains out of molehills." In other words, "Don't exaggerate the difficulty when you haven't yet tried to climb that particular hill." Most obstacles are surmountable if one truly tries, prays and does not overestimate the opposition.

Matthew 17:20b
[20b] "Truly I tell you, if you have faith as small as a mustard seed, you can say to this mountain, 'Move from here to there,' and it will move. Nothing will be impossible for you."

Ephesians 6:10-11
[10] Finally, be strong in the Lord and in his mighty power. [11] Put on the full armor of God, so that you can take your stand against the devil's schemes.

Philippians 4:13
[13] I can do all this through him who gives me strength.

James 4:7
[7] Submit yourselves, then, to God. Resist the devil, and he will flee from you.

Prayer Guide
Our holy, heavenly Father, may your will prevail. Supply our daily needs. Forgive our sins as we forgive others. Protect us from temptation and rescue us from evil. We pray through the name, power and blood of our Lord, Jesus. Amen.

Enough?

When our day, week, life is too much for us, we may exclaim, "Enough is enough!" meaning, "I can't take this pain, stress, conflict...whatever the issue...anymore!" Contrast the end of our rope with the promises of God. That will be enough.

Deuteronomy 31:6,8
[6] "Be strong and courageous. Do not be afraid or terrified because of them, for the LORD your God goes with you; he will never leave you nor forsake you."

[8] "The LORD himself goes before you and will be with you; he will never leave you nor forsake you. Do not be afraid; do not be discouraged."

Hebrews 6:18-19a
[18] God did this so that, by two unchangeable things in which it is impossible for God to lie, we who have fled to take hold of the hope set before us may be greatly encouraged. [19] We have this hope as an anchor for the soul, firm and secure.

Prayer Guide
Our holy, heavenly Father, may your will prevail. Supply our daily needs. Forgive our sins as we forgive others. Protect us from temptation and rescue us from evil. We pray through the name, power and blood of our Lord, Jesus. Amen.

Forgiveness

Forgiveness, in God's way of defining it, is a hard concept for many of us. It is saying and really meaning that we no longer hold another responsible for sins he has committed against us. That is not what we want! We want repentance…we want the sinner to beg for our forgiveness and acknowledge that he/she has done wrong against us. We may even want some sort of repayment…a penance, if you will. It is not natural simply to say, "I forgive you, no strings attached. You did wrong, but I am choosing to let you go free—you no longer owe me a debt." No, this is not natural—this is supernatural. The ones who end up being freed the most are the ones who have been injured. The sinner still must answer to God for what he has done. If the sinner realizes and admits his sin, asking God to forgive, then God himself will also set the sinner free.

Matthew 6:12-14
[12] 'And forgive us our debts,
    as we also have forgiven our debtors.
[13] And lead us not into temptation,
    but deliver us from the evil one.'
[14] For if you forgive other people when they sin against you, your heavenly Father will also forgive you.

Romans 5:8
[8] But God demonstrates his own love for us in this: While we were still sinners, Christ died for us.

Prayer Guide
Our holy, heavenly Father, may your will prevail. Supply our daily needs. Forgive our sins as we forgive others. Protect us from temptation and rescue us from evil. We pray through the name, power and blood of our Lord, Jesus. Amen.

Impossible Requirements

Does it seem like some commands in the Bible are simply impossible to obey? If we are unable to obey, then why does God tell us to do these things? Maybe it is so we will discover the only way to be obedient is by drawing on God's strength. Our own resources are utterly feeble in the face of life's difficulties.

John 15:5
[5] "I am the vine; you are the branches. If you remain in me and I in you, you will bear much fruit; apart from me you can do nothing."

1 Thessalonians 5:16-18
[16] Rejoice always, [17] pray continually, [18] give thanks in all circumstances; for this is God's will for you in Christ Jesus.

Prayer Guide
Our holy, heavenly Father, may your will prevail. Supply our daily needs. Forgive our sins as we forgive others. Protect us from temptation and rescue us from evil. We pray through the name, power and blood of our Lord, Jesus. Amen.

Listen Up!

Are we paying attention to God? He is speaking to us in the Bible, through the stormy winds and waves, as well as in good and pleasant times.

Matthew 13:15
[15] 'For this people's heart has become calloused;
they hardly hear with their ears,
and they have closed their eyes.
Otherwise they might see with their eyes,
hear with their ears,
understand with their hearts
and turn, and I would heal them.'

1 Corinthians 10:23-24
[23] "I have the right to do anything," you say—but not everything is beneficial. "I have the right to do anything"—but not everything is constructive. [24] No one should seek their own good, but the good of others.

Prayer Guide
Our holy, heavenly Father, may your will prevail. Supply our daily needs. Forgive our sins as we forgive others. Protect us from temptation and rescue us from evil. We pray through the name, power and blood of our Lord, Jesus. Amen.

Mental Mud

Negative or sinful thought patterns are similar to the ruts in a dirt road during spring mud season in New England. Once you slide into those tracks you're pretty much stuck in them. It takes outside intervention in the form of a work crew scraping the ruts smooth with a road grader and pouring on a good layer of gravel for the driver to regain control. To get out of our negative thought ruts into more positive and God-pleasing ones requires awareness and the reinforcement of God's word and the counsel of mature Christians.

Romans 8:6-8
[6] The mind governed by the flesh is death, but the mind governed by the Spirit is life and peace. [7] The mind governed by the flesh is hostile to God; it does not submit to God's law, nor can it do so. [8] Those who are in the realm of the flesh cannot please God.

Colossians 3:5,8-10
[5] Put to death, therefore, whatever belongs to your earthly nature: sexual immorality, impurity, lust, evil desires and greed, which is idolatry.

[8] But now you must also rid yourselves of all such things as these: anger, rage, malice, slander, and filthy language from your lips. [9] Do not lie to each other, since you have taken off your old self with its practices [10] and have put on the new self, which is being renewed in knowledge in the image of its Creator.

1 Thessalonians 4:7-8
[7] For God did not call us to be impure, but to live a holy life.
[8] Therefore, anyone who rejects this instruction does not reject a human being but God, the very God who gives you his Holy Spirit.

Prayer Guide
Our holy, heavenly Father, may your will prevail. Supply our daily needs. Forgive our sins as we forgive others. Protect us from temptation and rescue us from evil. We pray through the name, power and blood of our Lord, Jesus. Amen.

Peace

Peace is in scarce supply these days, both on the personal and the global fronts. It is not a quality that we can create on our own, nor has the world community figured out how to obtain it. When the turmoil of our world threatens to overwhelm us, we need to learn that true peace of heart and mind is a gift from God. It is not to be found so much as it is to be accepted. Jesus told his disciples (and therefore us, if we too are followers of Christ) that he would give us peace.

John 14:27
[27] Peace I leave with you; my peace I give you. I do not give to you as the world gives. Do not let your hearts be troubled and do not be afraid.

John 16:33
[33] "I have told you these things, so that in me you may have peace. In this world you will have trouble. But take heart! I have overcome the world."

Prayer Guide

Our holy, heavenly Father, may your will prevail. Supply our daily needs. Forgive our sins as we forgive others. Protect us from temptation and rescue us from evil. We pray through the name, power and blood of our Lord, Jesus. Amen.

Read and Heed

If you have ever gotten a speeding ticket, you know ignorance of the law is no excuse. Maybe you really did not notice the speed limit, or more likely you were not paying close attention to the speedometer. Perhaps you were even intentionally going too fast. The "why" doesn't matter—the fact remains that you (and I) have broken the law. In other areas of life, we need to read and heed the directions. The Bible is God's instruction book for every individual. Before all else fails, READ and FOLLOW the instructions! It will save a lot of time and prevent heartache. However, when we fail, as we all do at times, God is ready to forgive us. All we need to do is ask him, our loving, heavenly Father.

Psalm 103:11-12
11   For as high as the heavens are above the earth,
       so great is his love for those who fear him;
12   as far as the east is from the west,
       so far has he removed our transgressions from us.

2 Timothy 3:16-17
[16] All Scripture is God-breathed and is useful for teaching, rebuking, correcting and training in righteousness, [17] so that the servant of God may be thoroughly equipped for every good work.

Hebrews 4:12
[12] For the word of God is alive and active. Sharper than any double-edged sword, it penetrates even to dividing soul and spirit, joints and marrow; it judges the thoughts and attitudes of the heart.

Prayer Guide
Our holy, heavenly Father, may your will prevail. Supply our daily needs. Forgive our sins as we forgive others. Protect us from temptation and rescue us from evil. We pray through the name, power and blood of our Lord, Jesus. Amen.

Seeking Success

Secular gurus tout power and self-confidence as keys to success. People take classes and read all sorts of how-to manuals in a search for the elusive goal we term "success." The Bible has story after story illustrating weak people finding victory through a strong God. Our acknowledgment of our personal inability to overcome obstacles without God's help or intervention is the path to real and eternal success. Perhaps we should examine what we believe to be true success.

Psalm 21:1,7

1   The king rejoices in your strength, LORD.
       How great is his joy in the victories you give!

7   For the king trusts in the LORD;
       through the unfailing love of the Most High
       he will not be shaken.

2 Corinthians 12:10

[10] That is why, for Christ's sake, I delight in weaknesses, in insults, in hardships, in persecutions, in difficulties. For when I am weak, then I am strong.

1 Peter 5:6

[6] Humble yourselves, therefore, under God's mighty hand, that he may lift you up in due time.

Prayer Guide

Our holy, heavenly Father, may your will prevail. Supply our daily needs. Forgive our sins as we forgive others. Protect us from temptation and rescue us from evil. We pray through the name, power and blood of our Lord, Jesus. Amen.

Tending to Disorder

A principle of physics known as entropy states that order inevitably yields to disorder. In simple language, this means things wear out. Humans get old and die. This is a fact. But our spirits rise above scientific facts. Our real inner selves—our souls—will live on in a new heavenly dimension through God's power.

2 Corinthians 4:16-18
[16] Therefore we do not lose heart. Though outwardly we are wasting away, yet inwardly we are being renewed day by day. [17] For our light and momentary troubles are achieving for us an eternal glory that far outweighs them all. [18] So we fix our eyes not on what is seen, but on what is unseen, since what is seen is temporary, but what is unseen is eternal.

Prayer Guide
Our holy, heavenly Father, may your will prevail. Supply our daily needs. Forgive our sins as we forgive others. Protect us from temptation and rescue us from evil. We pray through the name, power and blood of our Lord, Jesus. Amen.

Trust or Fear?

Most of us are afraid of some things. Some of us are afraid of most things. Why? It is probably because we are not in control, but we want to be. God's word tells us repeatedly not to be afraid, not to fear and not to worry. Whether we die in an accident at age eight or in our sleep at ninety-eight, we are in the Lord's hands. Fear and worry will not help or change anything. Trusting in God will help everything.

Psalm 56:3-4
[3] When I am afraid,
  I put my trust in you.
[4] In God, whose word I praise—
  in God I trust and am not afraid.
  What can mere mortals do to me?

Psalm 146:3
[3] Do not put your trust in princes,
  in human beings, who cannot save.

Matthew 6:27
[27] Can any one of you by worrying add a single hour to your life?

Prayer Guide
Our holy, heavenly Father, may your will prevail. Supply our daily needs. Forgive our sins as we forgive others. Protect us from temptation and rescue us from evil. We pray through the name, power and blood of our Lord, Jesus. Amen.

Where Is My Help?

When our enemies (real or imagined) loom large, where do we find help? It seems obvious, but if it were, we would not fear. We get help from God. Remember, the power above all powers is on our side.

Psalm 120:1
1   I call on the LORD in my distress,
        and he answers me.

Psalm 121:1-2
1   I lift up my eyes to the mountains—
        where does my help come from?
2   My help comes from the LORD,
        the Maker of heaven and earth.

Ephesians 6:13
[13] Therefore put on the full armor of God, so that when the day of evil comes, you may be able to stand your ground, and after you have done everything, to stand.

Prayer Guide
Our holy, heavenly Father, may your will prevail. Supply our daily needs. Forgive our sins as we forgive others. Protect us from temptation and rescue us from evil. We pray through the name, power and blood of our Lord, Jesus. Amen.

Chapter 4

Accept Your Gifts 50

"Big Bang" or Big God? 51

Count Your Blessings 52

Even If... 53

Give a Good Word. 54

In a Storm 55

Locked Doors 56

Music for Our Souls. 57

Peace Enables Life 58

Real Wealth. 59

Self-confidence 60

The Concept of Time. 61

Truth in Love 62

Where to Turn? 63

Accept Your Gifts

God gives us many gifts throughout our lives. He offers us the free gift of salvation through the sacrifice of his son, Jesus. He lavishes us with unconditional love. He offers hope and many promises. He even gives us the faith to believe in Him. He also gives us spiritual gifts enabling us to serve in various capacities. However, gifts are not worth much unless we accept and use them. His gifts are precious, even if some include big responsibilities. We don't get to choose what or when God gives, only to accept or reject what he gives us.

Romans 12:6-8
[6] We have different gifts, according to the grace given to each of us. If your gift is prophesying, then prophesy in accordance with your faith; [7] if it is serving, then serve; if it is teaching, then teach; [8] if it is to encourage, then give encouragement; if it is giving, then give generously; if it is to lead, do it diligently; if it is to show mercy, do it cheerfully.

1 Corinthians 12:4-6
[4] There are different kinds of gifts, but the same Spirit distributes them. [5] There are different kinds of service, but the same Lord. [6] There are different kinds of working, but in all of them and in everyone it is the same God at work.

Ephesians 2:8-10
[8] For it is by grace you have been saved, through faith—and this is not from yourselves, it is the gift of God—[9] not by works, so that no one can boast. [10] For we are God's handiwork, created in Christ Jesus to do good works, which God prepared in advance for us to do.

Prayer Guide
Our holy, heavenly Father, may your will prevail. Supply our daily needs. Forgive our sins as we forgive others. Protect us from temptation and rescue us from evil. We pray through the name, power and blood of our Lord, Jesus. Amen.

"Big Bang" or Big God?

Even the smartest scientist cannot explain the beginning of the universe. If there were a "Big Bang" as many believe, where did the elements come from to create the explosion? With all the amassed knowledge of the ages, there is more we do not know than what we do know. It is wisest to look to the eternal God for answers to all our questions. Chances are he will not answer all of them; we will have to wait for heaven for complete understanding. But his answers are better than man's.

Genesis 9:13,15

13 I have set my rainbow in the clouds, and it will be the sign of the covenant between me and the earth.

15 I will remember my covenant between me and you and all living creatures of every kind. Never again will the waters become a flood to destroy all life.

Job 38:2-7

2 "Who is this that obscures my plans
　　with words without knowledge?
3 Brace yourself like a man;
　　I will question you,
　　and you shall answer me.
4 "Where were you when I laid the earth's foundation?
　　Tell me, if you understand.
5 Who marked off its dimensions? Surely you know!
　　Who stretched a measuring line across it?
6 On what were its footings set,
　　or who laid its cornerstone—
7 while the morning stars sang together
　　and all the angels shouted for joy?"

Prayer Guide
Our holy, heavenly Father, may your will prevail. Supply our daily needs. Forgive our sins as we forgive others. Protect us from temptation and rescue us from evil. We pray through the name, power and blood of our Lord, Jesus. Amen.

Count Your Blessings

We too often number our negatives. It is so much better to count our blessings. Get a notebook and write them down or list them in the computer. It is too easy to recall what is wrong. Record what is right... day by day.

Psalm 103:1-2
1   Praise the LORD, my soul;
       all my inmost being, praise his holy name.
2   Praise the LORD, my soul,
       and forget not all his benefits—

Lamentations 3:31-32
31   For no one is cast off
       by the Lord forever.
32   Though he brings grief, he will show compassion,
       so great is his unfailing love.

Prayer Guide

Our holy, heavenly Father, may your will prevail. Supply our daily needs. Forgive our sins as we forgive others. Protect us from temptation and rescue us from evil. We pray through the name, power and blood of our Lord, Jesus. Amen.

Even If...

Even though the world is in turmoil and maybe our family is feuding and/or our health is questionable, we can have hope. God is bigger than all the negatives we see. He can help us refocus and begin to see the positives of the here and now, as well as the yet to come.

Psalm 16:8-9
8   I keep my eyes always on the Lord.
      With him at my right hand, I will not be shaken.
9   Therefore my heart is glad and my tongue rejoices;
      my body also will rest secure,

Habakkuk 3:17-18
17   Though the fig tree does not bud
      and there are no grapes on the vines,
    though the olive crop fails
      and the fields produce no food,
    though there are no sheep in the pen
      and no cattle in the stalls,
18   yet I will rejoice in the Lord,
      I will be joyful in God my Savior.

Philippians 4:7
7 And the peace of God, which transcends all understanding, will guard your hearts and your minds in Christ Jesus.

Prayer Guide
Our holy, heavenly Father, may your will prevail. Supply our daily needs. Forgive our sins as we forgive others. Protect us from temptation and rescue us from evil. We pray through the name, power and blood of our Lord, Jesus. Amen.

Give a Good Word

Good words build up, while bad ones break down. This is true whether we are listening or speaking. We have no control over what others say, but we can discipline what comes out of our own mouths. Remember how good it feels to be encouraged. Whereas criticism can replay in our minds and hurt us for a very long time, a compliment or helpful phrase can lift us up for days.

Ephesians 4:29
[29] Do not let any unwholesome talk come out of your mouths, but only what is helpful for building others up according to their needs, that it may benefit those who listen.

James 1:26
[26] Those who consider themselves religious and yet do not keep a tight rein on their tongues deceive themselves, and their religion is worthless.

1 Peter 3:10
[10] For,
> "Whoever would love life
> and see good days
> must keep their tongue from evil
> and their lips from deceitful speech."

Prayer Guide
Our holy, heavenly Father, may your will prevail. Supply our daily needs. Forgive our sins as we forgive others. Protect us from temptation and rescue us from evil. We pray through the name, power and blood of our Lord, Jesus. Amen.

In a Storm

If we are in a boat that's rocking with life's storms, threatening to swamp us, take heart—Jesus is in the boat with us, and he can calm the storm. No matter how rough the waters surrounding us, our boat will not sink. Do not fear! Exercise faith. Like our muscles, our faith will not grow stronger without stress.

Matthew 6:31-33
[31] So do not worry, saying, 'What shall we eat?' or 'What shall we drink?' or 'What shall we wear?' [32] For the pagans run after all these things, and your heavenly Father knows that you need them. [33] But seek first his kingdom and his righteousness, and all these things will be given to you as well.

Matthew 14:29-31
[29] "Come," he said.
Then Peter got down out of the boat, walked on the water and came toward Jesus. [30] But when he saw the wind, he was afraid and, beginning to sink, cried out, "Lord, save me!"
[31] Immediately Jesus reached out his hand and caught him. "You of little faith," he said, "why did you doubt?"

Luke 8:23-25
[23] As they sailed, he fell asleep. A squall came down on the lake, so that the boat was being swamped, and they were in great danger. [24] The disciples went and woke him, saying, "Master, Master, we're going to drown!"
He got up and rebuked the wind and the raging waters; the storm subsided, and all was calm. [25] "Where is your faith?" he asked his disciples.
In fear and amazement they asked one another, "Who is this? He commands even the winds and the water, and they obey him."

Prayer Guide
Our holy, heavenly Father, may your will prevail. Supply our daily needs. Forgive our sins as we forgive others. Protect us from temptation and rescue us from evil. We pray through the name, power and blood of our Lord, Jesus. Amen.

Locked Doors

What shall we do when every door seems locked and every window bolted shut? We need to acknowledge that we may have locked them ourselves to prevent intrusion. When God blocks a passageway from his side, it is to keep us from going the wrong way. He is all about protecting us from destructive decisions. We must figure out who has locked the door.

Psalm 73:25-26
[25] Whom have I in heaven but you?
And earth has nothing I desire besides you.
[26] My flesh and my heart may fail,
but God is the strength of my heart
and my portion forever.

Proverbs 16:25
[25] There is a way that appears to be right,
but in the end it leads to death.

Prayer Guide
Our holy, heavenly Father, may your will prevail. Supply our daily needs. Forgive our sins as we forgive others. Protect us from temptation and rescue us from evil. We pray through the name, power and blood of our Lord, Jesus. Amen.

Music for Our Souls

Even if we are not musically inclined, we know music can soothe and heal. So choose music with words of comfort and truth. Or choose instrumentals that remind you of good things. The Psalms in the Bible were written to be sung. Unfortunately, they didn't pass along the tunes. Nevertheless, they contain words of praise, regret for sins, despair over difficulties and affirmation of ultimate victory through God's mighty power.

Many people shed tears when our national anthem is played or sung. We all know the meaning behind the mournful bugle playing "Taps," and people from many lands know the significance of "Amazing Grace," written by a repentant ship captain/slave trader when he came to understand the love, grace and forgiveness of God. If you cannot carry a tune, at least listen and make a joyful sound of praise.

Psalm 95:1-2
1   Come, let us sing for joy to the Lord;
       let us shout aloud to the Rock of our salvation.
2   Let us come before him with thanksgiving
       and extol him with music and song.

Psalm 100:1-2
1   Shout for joy to the Lord, all the earth.
2   Worship the Lord with gladness;
       come before him with joyful songs.

Prayer Guide
Our holy, heavenly Father, may your will prevail. Supply our daily needs. Forgive our sins as we forgive others. Protect us from temptation and rescue us from evil. We pray through the name, power and blood of our Lord, Jesus. Amen.

Peace Enables Life

Until we find peace in knowing that God will carry us through death, we will not do very well with life. We must see the big picture in order to be aware of the small, daily glimpses of God's power, grace, love and mercy.

Isaiah 12:2
2 "Surely God is my salvation;
I will trust and not be afraid.
The Lord, the Lord himself, is my strength and my defense;
he has become my salvation."

Isaiah 26:3-4
3 You will keep in perfect peace
those whose minds are steadfast,
because they trust in you.
4 Trust in the Lord forever,
for the Lord, the Lord himself, is the Rock eternal.

Romans 5:1-5
[1] Therefore, since we have been justified through faith, we have peace with God through our Lord Jesus Christ, [2] through whom we have gained access by faith into this grace in which we now stand. And we boast in the hope of the glory of God. [3] Not only so, but we also glory in our sufferings, because we know that suffering produces perseverance; [4] perseverance, character; and character, hope. [5] And hope does not put us to shame, because God's love has been poured out into our hearts through the Holy Spirit, who has been given to us.

Prayer Guide
Our holy, heavenly Father, may your will prevail. Supply our daily needs. Forgive our sins as we forgive others. Protect us from temptation and rescue us from evil. We pray through the name, power and blood of our Lord, Jesus. Amen.

Real Wealth

What is truly valuable? If a fat bank account and costly possessions were the real measure of wealth, we would not hear of so many suicides by the rich and famous. It is not money that matters the most—it is peace of mind, faith, hope and love.

Romans 15:13
[13] May the God of hope fill you with all joy and peace as you trust in him, so that you may overflow with hope by the power of the Holy Spirit.

1 Timothy 6:6-9
[6] But godliness with contentment is great gain. [7] For we brought nothing into the world, and we can take nothing out of it. [8] But if we have food and clothing, we will be content with that. [9] Those who want to get rich fall into temptation and a trap and into many foolish and harmful desires that plunge people into ruin and destruction.

1 Peter 1:3-5
[3] Praise be to the God and Father of our Lord Jesus Christ! In his great mercy he has given us new birth into a living hope through the resurrection of Jesus Christ from the dead, [4] and into an inheritance that can never perish, spoil or fade. This inheritance is kept in heaven for you, [5] who through faith are shielded by God's power until the coming of the salvation that is ready to be revealed in the last time.

Prayer Guide
Our holy, heavenly Father, may your will prevail. Supply our daily needs. Forgive our sins as we forgive others. Protect us from temptation and rescue us from evil. We pray through the name, power and blood of our Lord, Jesus. Amen.

Self-confidence

Many of us suffer from low self-esteem and we lack self-confidence. It is good to be aware of our own weaknesses, but we must recognize they don't have to be permanent. If we depend only on our personal abilities, we are guaranteed to fail at some point. But when our dependence is on God, we ultimately succeed—even when we fail. When we study his word and grow in our faith, we will find our esteem and confidence in him—and that's a much better place to find it.

Romans 12:3
[3] For by the grace given me I say to every one of you: Do not think of yourself more highly than you ought, but rather think of yourself with sober judgment, in accordance with the faith God has distributed to each of you.

2 Corinthians 3:5
[5] Not that we are competent in ourselves to claim anything for ourselves, but our competence comes from God.

Prayer Guide
Our holy, heavenly Father, may your will prevail. Supply our daily needs. Forgive our sins as we forgive others. Protect us from temptation and rescue us from evil. We pray through the name, power and blood of our Lord, Jesus. Amen.

The Concept of Time

A moment of sorrow can seem to last an eternity, while a moment of joy may seem so fleeting we want to catch it and stop the clock. We all experience these extremes and wonder about the entire concept of time. When our own or another's pain persists, we want it to end right now! If the emotion is good, we try to make it last. We acknowledge God has complete power over all time as well as our perception of it. When we recognize this as part of God's sovereignty, we can learn through difficulties as well as pleasures. We can find real and eternal joy in his strength within good and bad circumstances.

Psalm 13:1-2,5

1 How long, Lord? Will you forget me forever?
   How long will you hide your face from me?
2 How long must I wrestle with my thoughts
   and day after day have sorrow in my heart?
   How long will my enemy triumph over me?

5 But I trust in your unfailing love;
   my heart rejoices in your salvation.

Ecclesiastes 3:1,11

1 There is a time for everything,
   and a season for every activity under the heavens:

[11] He has made everything beautiful in its time. He has also set eternity in the human heart; yet no one can fathom what God has done from beginning to end.

Prayer Guide
Our holy, heavenly Father, may your will prevail. Supply our daily needs. Forgive our sins as we forgive others. Protect us from temptation and rescue us from evil. We pray through the name, power and blood of our Lord, Jesus. Amen.

Truth in Love

Sister, brother, parent, child, spouse, friend—those we love the most often hurt us the most. We in turn either spout off hasty words, or we stuff the pain deep inside, where it causes greater wounds than the initial offense. Our desire for perfect, or at least pleasant, relationships dissipates in the daily brew of reality. We cannot change others' words or perceptions...so what are we to do? The only thing we can do: be responsible for our own words and reactions.

Ephesians 4:15,25-27,29
[15] Instead, speaking the truth in love, we will grow to become in every respect the mature body of him who is the head, that is, Christ.

[25] Therefore each of you must put off falsehood and speak truthfully to your neighbor, for we are all members of one body. [26] "In your anger do not sin": Do not let the sun go down while you are still angry, [27] and do not give the devil a foothold.

[29] Do not let any unwholesome talk come out of your mouths, but only what is helpful for building others up according to their needs, that it may benefit those who listen.

Prayer Guide
Our holy, heavenly Father, may your will prevail. Supply our daily needs. Forgive our sins as we forgive others. Protect us from temptation and rescue us from evil. We pray through the name, power and blood of our Lord, Jesus. Amen.

Where to Turn?

When everything seems dark and frightening, where do we turn? Friends and family may care, but they seldom have the power to make life better...whether the problem is physical or emotional. So once again we turn to God, who is our ultimate answer.

Romans 8:31-32
[31] What, then, shall we say in response to these things? If God is for us, who can be against us? [32] He who did not spare his own Son, but gave him up for us all—how will he not also, along with him, graciously give us all things?

Romans 15:13
[13] May the God of hope fill you with all joy and peace as you trust in him, so that you may overflow with hope by the power of the Holy Spirit.

Prayer Guide
Our holy, heavenly Father, may your will prevail. Supply our daily needs. Forgive our sins as we forgive others. Protect us from temptation and rescue us from evil. We pray through the name, power and blood of our Lord, Jesus. Amen.

Chapter 5

Boundaries 66

Dependence 67

Evils We See 68

Giving Due Credit 69

Help Yourself 70

Inaction 71

Look Above 72

My Way or His? 73

Perseverance Trumps Preference 74

Regrets 75

Self-Pity 76

The End of My Rope 77

Tug of War 78

Who Really Knows? 79

Boundaries

What are appropriate boundaries to set to protect oneself from the sins of others? The principle of Scripture is that we do not condone sin nor allow it to go on against us without any protest unless there is a higher reason. Jesus threw the moneychangers from the temple because they were making a mockery of God's house, yet he turned his cheek to be struck again and again when he was accused falsely of blasphemy by the high priest before the crucifixion. The former was to stop blasphemy against the true sacrifices to God; the latter was to fulfill prophecy.

Matthew 18:15-17
[15] "If your brother or sister sins, go and point out their fault, just between the two of you. If they listen to you, you have won them over. [16] But if they will not listen, take one or two others along, so that 'every matter may be established by the testimony of two or three witnesses.' [17] If they still refuse to listen, tell it to the church; and if they refuse to listen even to the church, treat them as you would a pagan or a tax collector."

Matthew 21:13
[13] "It is written," he said to them, "'My house will be called a house of prayer,' but you are making it 'a den of robbers.'"

Matthew 26:65-68
[65] Then the high priest tore his clothes and said, "He has spoken blasphemy! Why do we need any more witnesses? Look, now you have heard the blasphemy. [66] What do you think?"
"He is worthy of death," they answered.
[67] Then they spit in his face and struck him with their fists. Others slapped him [68] and said, "Prophesy to us, Messiah. Who hit you?

Prayer Guide
Our holy, heavenly Father, may your will prevail. Supply our daily needs. Forgive our sins as we forgive others. Protect us from temptation and rescue us from evil. We pray through the name, power and blood of our Lord, Jesus. Amen.

Dependence

So often we are like a stubborn toddler, pouting and stating emphatically, "I do it myself!" The fact is, most often we cannot do it ourselves. We need to acknowledge our need for God's strength and direction. We very much need to put his wisdom and will first, not last!

Psalm 62:8
8   Trust in him at all times, you people;
      pour out your hearts to him,
      for God is our refuge.

Psalm 63:6-8
6   On my bed I remember you;
      I think of you through the watches of the night.
7   Because you are my help,
      I sing in the shadow of your wings.
8   I cling to you;
      your right hand upholds me.

Titus 2:11-14
[11] For the grace of God has appeared that offers salvation to all people. [12] It teaches us to say "No" to ungodliness and worldly passions, and to live self-controlled, upright and godly lives in this present age, [13] while we wait for the blessed hope—the appearing of the glory of our great God and Savior, Jesus Christ, [14] who gave himself for us to redeem us from all wickedness and to purify for himself a people that are his very own, eager to do what is good.

Prayer Guide
Our holy, heavenly Father, may your will prevail. Supply our daily needs. Forgive our sins as we forgive others. Protect us from temptation and rescue us from evil. We pray through the name, power and blood of our Lord, Jesus. Amen.

Evils We See

The evils of inhumane massacres reported on TV frighten and horrify us all. What can we do in the face of such barbarism? Perhaps we cannot do very much. We should be aware this was foretold from the time of Christ, and it continues to this present day. What we can do is pray and live as close to Christ as possible so that by life or death, we are living the love he modeled.

Deuteronomy 31:6
[6] "Be strong and courageous. Do not be afraid or terrified because of them, for the Lord your God goes with you; he will never leave you nor forsake you."

Matthew 24:12-13
[12] Because of the increase of wickedness, the love of most will grow cold, [13] but the one who stands firm to the end will be saved.

Prayer Guide
Our holy, heavenly Father, may your will prevail. Supply our daily needs. Forgive our sins as we forgive others. Protect us from temptation and rescue us from evil. We pray through the name, power and blood of our Lord, Jesus. Amen.

Giving Due Credit

Remember to give God credit for all that is good and to blame Satan for lies, deceit and disasters. How sad that we often blame God when tragedy strikes. We need to learn the difference between God's perfect will, which includes all that is good, and his permissive will, which allows the brokenness of our world and all its sadness to continue—for now. However, though difficulties will continue, we can rest in the promise that God will bring good out of even the hardest situations.

1 Chronicles 16:34
[34] Give thanks to the Lord, for he is good;
his love endures forever.

Malachi 3:17-18
[17] "On the day when I act," says the Lord Almighty, "they will be my treasured possession. I will spare them, just as a father has compassion and spares his son who serves him. [18] And you will again see the distinction between the righteous and the wicked, between those who serve God and those who do not."

Matthew 7:11
[11] If you, then, though you are evil, know how to give good gifts to your children, how much more will your Father in heaven give good gifts to those who ask him!

Romans 8:28
[28] And we know that in all things God works for the good of those who love him, who have been called according to his purpose.

Prayer Guide

Our holy, heavenly Father, may your will prevail. Supply our daily needs. Forgive our sins as we forgive others. Protect us from temptation and rescue us from evil. We pray through the name, power and blood of our Lord, Jesus. Amen.

Help Yourself

The media gives great emphasis to the importance of good nutrition and of "self" care. Experts have proven our mental, emotional and physical well-being are closely linked. Inadequate intake of needed nutrients, insufficient sleep, limited physical activity, infrequent interaction with others and increased stress can eventually lead to illness and disease. But what science does not acknowledge is the role spiritual health plays in our overall well-being. We were designed to connect with one another. Even more importantly, we were intended to be in relationship with God. Yet many neglect a close fellowship with the creator. Starving ourselves spiritually—more than any other way—usually leads to all sorts of maladies—which are expressed in dysfunctional relationships, mental health issues and sin. It is imperative to feed our inner persons with every element we need.

Acts 2:42,46-47a
[42] They devoted themselves to the apostles' teaching and to fellowship, to the breaking of bread and to prayer.

[46] Every day they continued to meet together in the temple courts. They broke bread in their homes and ate together with glad and sincere hearts, [47] praising God and enjoying the favor of all the people.

1 Corinthians 3:2-3
[2] I gave you milk, not solid food, for you were not yet ready for it. Indeed, you are still not ready. [3] You are still worldly. For since there is jealousy and quarreling among you, are you not worldly? Are you not acting like mere humans?

Titus 2:11-12
[11] For the grace of God has appeared that offers salvation to all people. [12] It teaches us to say "No" to ungodliness and worldly passions, and to live self-controlled, upright and godly lives in this present age,

Prayer Guide

Our holy, heavenly Father, may your will prevail. Supply our daily needs. Forgive our sins as we forgive others. Protect us from temptation and rescue us from evil. We pray through the name, power and blood of our Lord, Jesus. Amen.

Inaction

Doing nothing is a negative decision...unless it's consciously choosing to withdraw and be still in prayer to listen to God. When paralysis and inaction come from fear, it seems like some part of our inner being dies. However, Jesus Christ is the Lord of the resurrection. He wants us to live now and into eternity.

Mark 9:24
[24] Immediately the boy's father exclaimed, "I do believe; help me overcome my unbelief!"

John 20:30-31
[30] Jesus performed many other signs in the presence of his disciples, which are not recorded in this book. [31] But these are written that you may believe that Jesus is the Messiah, the Son of God, and that by believing you may have life in his name.

Acts 1:3
[3] After his suffering, he presented himself to them and gave many convincing proofs that he was alive. He appeared to them over a period of forty days and spoke about the kingdom of God.

Prayer Guide
Our holy, heavenly Father, may your will prevail. Supply our daily needs. Forgive our sins as we forgive others. Protect us from temptation and rescue us from evil. We pray through the name, power and blood of our Lord, Jesus. Amen.

Look Above

Everyone has a battle (or battles) he or she is currently fighting or storms we've already been through. It is not "if" we'll face trials, it is "when." The world is broken and so are we. Only God defeats the enemy, controls the storms and gives meaning to our stories. Therefore, look above the circumstances and find answers in God and his word.

Psalm 102:19-20

[19] "The LORD looked down from his sanctuary on high,
from heaven he viewed the earth,
[20] to hear the groans of the prisoners
and release those condemned to death."

Romans 15:13

[13] May the God of hope fill you with all joy and peace as you trust in him, so that you may overflow with hope by the power of the Holy Spirit.

Prayer Guide

Our holy, heavenly Father, may your will prevail. Supply our daily needs. Forgive our sins as we forgive others. Protect us from temptation and rescue us from evil. We pray through the name, power and blood of our Lord, Jesus. Amen.

My Way or His?

We rush around doing all we think is necessary. A lot of our activities and work truly are important. Yet wisdom and balance are absolutely vital. Finding time and peace in the Lord is a personal choice—a matter of reordering priorities. It's not impossible, but you do have to be intentional.

Psalm 25:4-5

4 Show me your ways, Lord,
    teach me your paths.
5 Guide me in your truth and teach me,
    for you are God my Savior,
    and my hope is in you all day long.

Psalm 27:13-14

13 I remain confident of this:
    I will see the goodness of the Lord
    in the land of the living.
14 Wait for the Lord;
    be strong and take heart
    and wait for the Lord.

Proverbs 23:4-5

4 Do not wear yourself out to get rich;
    do not trust your own cleverness.
5 Cast but a glance at riches, and they are gone,
    for they will surely sprout wings
    and fly off to the sky like an eagle.

Prayer Guide
Our holy, heavenly Father, may your will prevail. Supply our daily needs. Forgive our sins as we forgive others. Protect us from temptation and rescue us from evil. We pray through the name, power and blood of our Lord, Jesus. Amen.

Perseverance Trumps Preference

Most of us do not mature or change our behavior when everything goes smoothly, yet we do not like enduring difficulties. However, the hard times have a way of changing our priorities. Those with a seriously ill child or a declining parent are not absorbed with finding a new car, redecorating the house or buying fashionable clothes. None of those activities are inherently wrong, they just aren't so important when people are our top focus. When friends or loved ones have problems, we spend our energies seeking a cure or the best care available. When we let go of preferences, we learn how to persevere. Trials force us to choose: God's way or our way?

Hebrews 12:1-2
[1] Therefore, since we are surrounded by such a great cloud of witnesses, let us throw off everything that hinders and the sin that so easily entangles. And let us run with perseverance the race marked out for us, [2] fixing our eyes on Jesus, the pioneer and perfecter of faith. For the joy set before him he endured the cross, scorning its shame, and sat down at the right hand of the throne of God.

2 Peter 1:3,5-8
[3] His divine power has given us everything we need for a godly life through our knowledge of him who called us by his own glory and goodness.

[5] For this very reason, make every effort to add to your faith goodness; and to goodness, knowledge; [6] and to knowledge, self-control; and to self-control, perseverance; and to perseverance, godliness; [7] and to godliness, mutual affection; and to mutual affection, love. [8] For if you possess these qualities in increasing measure, they will keep you from being ineffective and unproductive in your knowledge of our Lord Jesus Christ.

Prayer Guide
Our holy, heavenly Father, may your will prevail. Supply our daily needs. Forgive our sins as we forgive others. Protect us from temptation and rescue us from evil. We pray through the name, power and blood of our Lord, Jesus. Amen.

Regrets

We can spend the present regretting our past. What a waste of the future! It is certainly possible to learn from our mistakes and the abuses of the past, but we must decide to move on. Sometimes that requires hard work, such as counseling, intense Bible study, or perhaps joining a support group. Certainly, God's help and determination are necessary to overcome sins committed against us or even by us. The more damage and abuse in our past, the more effort may be required to go forward with confidence. The big mistake is always looking back and never looking forward, as if we were trying to drive a car by looking in the rear-view mirror. How absurd! There are events and situations worth our grief, but healing can be achieved and joy experienced.

Lamentations 3:19-23, 55-58

19 I remember my affliction and my wandering,
   the bitterness and the gall.
20 I well remember them,
   and my soul is downcast within me.
21 Yet this I call to mind
   and therefore I have hope:
22 Because of the Lord's great love we are not consumed,
   for his compassions never fail.
23 They are new every morning;
   great is your faithfulness.
55 I called on your name, Lord,
   from the depths of the pit.
56 You heard my plea: "Do not close your ears
   to my cry for relief."
57 You came near when I called you,
   and you said, "Do not fear."
58 You, Lord, took up my case;
   you redeemed my life.

Prayer Guide
Our holy, heavenly Father, may your will prevail. Supply our daily needs. Forgive our sins as we forgive others. Protect us from temptation and rescue us from evil. We pray through the name, power and blood of our Lord, Jesus. Amen.

Self-Pity

Some of us seem to have more than our fair share of sorrows and trials. How did we ever get the idea that life is fair? Walk through an old graveyard and count the tombstones with children's names, and notice the ones with the same last names. Look for the year 1918 and see the clusters of family members who died. That was the year of the awful Spanish flu pandemic. Did you see the movie "Saving Private Ryan"? Why was it so important to protect him? Wasn't it because he was the last living son in that family? Man wants fairness, and he wants it in this life. That may be a noble thought, but it is not realistic. We wail "Why me, haven't I suffered enough?" There is a fine line between natural sorrow at our losses and accusing God of unfairness. God is always just and good—it's life in a fallen world that is unfair. We are responsible to treat everyone with fairness. We are accountable for the way we treat others, whether they deserve our goodwill or not.

Psalm 71:20

[20] Though you have made me see troubles,
many and bitter,
you will restore my life again;
from the depths of the earth
you will again bring me up.

Micah 6:8

[8] He has shown you, O mortal, what is good.
And what does the Lord require of you?
To act justly and to love mercy
and to walk humbly with your God.

Matthew 5:44

[44] But I tell you, love your enemies and pray for those who persecute you,

---

Prayer Guide

Our holy, heavenly Father, may your will prevail. Supply our daily needs. Forgive our sins as we forgive others. Protect us from temptation and rescue us from evil. We pray through the name, power and blood of our Lord, Jesus. Amen.

The End of My Rope

How often have I felt I am at the end of my rope and my grip is slipping? I've prayed, tried to trust, confessed sins and claimed forgiveness, but the problem stays right with me. I'm tired of the trouble and really don't understand why God doesn't seem to be helping. Reading the Psalms shows that I agree with the writers from thousands of years ago. God truly stays with me and guides me. He has my back.

Psalm 73:21-26

21 When my heart was grieved
   and my spirit embittered,
22 I was senseless and ignorant;
   I was a brute beast before you.
23 Yet I am always with you;
   you hold me by my right hand.
24 You guide me with your counsel,
   and afterward you will take me into glory.
25 Whom have I in heaven but you?
   And earth has nothing I desire besides you.
26 My flesh and my heart may fail,
   but God is the strength of my heart
   and my portion forever.

Psalm 77:7,10-11

7 "Will the Lord reject forever?
   Will he never show his favor again?"

10 Then I thought, "To this I will appeal:
   the years when the Most High stretched out his right hand.
11 I will remember the deeds of the Lord;
   yes, I will remember your miracles of long ago."

Prayer Guide

Our holy, heavenly Father, may your will prevail. Supply our daily needs. Forgive our sins as we forgive others. Protect us from temptation and rescue us from evil. We pray through the name, power and blood of our Lord, Jesus. Amen.

Tug of War

Life will always be a tug of war between good and evil. The problem is that people are in the middle, being jerked one way and then the other. We know who wins in the end, so we should align ourselves with God on the victor's side…but we should still expect to get a bit battered in the process.

Romans 7:21-25
[21] So I find this law at work: Although I want to do good, evil is right there with me. [22] For in my inner being I delight in God's law; [23] but I see another law at work in me, waging war against the law of my mind and making me a prisoner of the law of sin at work within me.
[24] What a wretched man I am! Who will rescue me from this body that is subject to death? [25] Thanks be to God, who delivers me through Jesus Christ our Lord! So then, I myself in my mind am a slave to God's law, but in my sinful nature a slave to the law of sin.

Prayer Guide
Our holy, heavenly Father, may your will prevail. Supply our daily needs. Forgive our sins as we forgive others. Protect us from temptation and rescue us from evil. We pray through the name, power and blood of our Lord, Jesus. Amen.

Who Really Knows?

Some pretty bright individuals dismiss the concept of a creator God with statements such as "It is all just nature or biology!" They discount divine intervention in daily life. But who really knows the truth? One can have extensive education and knowledge yet miss the wisdom of the ages. The smartest people know that they don't know it all. Let's be grateful for one who is higher, grander and more powerful than the finite human mind, as wonderful as it may be.

Genesis 1:27
[27] So God created mankind in his own image,
in the image of God he created them;
male and female he created them.

John 1:3-5
[3] Through him all things were made; without him nothing was made that has been made. [4] In him was life, and that life was the light of all mankind. [5] The light shines in the darkness, and the darkness has not overcome it.

Romans 1:20-23
[20] For since the creation of the world God's invisible qualities—his eternal power and divine nature—have been clearly seen, being understood from what has been made, so that people are without excuse.
[21] For although they knew God, they neither glorified him as God nor gave thanks to him, but their thinking became futile and their foolish hearts were darkened. [22] Although they claimed to be wise, they became fools [23] and exchanged the glory of the immortal God for images made to look like a mortal human being and birds and animals and reptiles.

Prayer Guide
Our holy, heavenly Father, may your will prevail. Supply our daily needs. Forgive our sins as we forgive others. Protect us from temptation and rescue us from evil. We pray through the name, power and blood of our Lord, Jesus. Amen.

Chapter 6

All or Nothing.........................82

Bridges 83

Desire or Dread?.................. 84

Exaggeration........................85

Goals..................................86

It Is God's Will 87

Look for Good 88

Need for 89

Power of Language 90

Rehash or Review................91

Self-what?...........................92

The Good Old Days..............93

Tunnel Vision.......................94

Whose Timing? 95

All or Nothing

Too often we are "all or nothing" people. Either we are annoyed by others, thinking our way is always best, or we have low self-esteem and habitually berate ourselves as being wrong or being a failure. These extremes are seldom accurate. We are valued children of God.

Philippians 2:3-4
[3] Do nothing out of selfish ambition or vain conceit. Rather, in humility value others above yourselves, [4] not looking to your own interests but each of you to the interests of the others.

Colossians 3:13
[13] Bear with each other and forgive one another if any of you has a grievance against someone. Forgive as the Lord forgave you.

Prayer Guide
Our holy, heavenly Father, may your will prevail. Supply our daily needs. Forgive our sins as we forgive others. Protect us from temptation and rescue us from evil. We pray through the name, power and blood of our Lord, Jesus. Amen.

Bridges

Bridges are connectors. They can connect one side of a chasm to another, or perhaps they simply go over a small dip that fills with rushing water when a storm hits. If they are strong, they can protect from disaster; if they are weak, they offer false security and then give way when needed most. Strong bridges are needed in relationships. They can be kind and loving words or actions. Bridges can be Scriptures that connect us to the truth and carry us safely to our destination. Jesus is the strongest bridge of all, conveying us from hopelessness to assurance across the deep pit of pain, disappointment and sin.

John 14:6
[6] Jesus answered, "I am the way and the truth and the life. No one comes to the Father except through me."

2 Thessalonians 2:16-17
[16] May our Lord Jesus Christ himself and God our Father, who loved us and by his grace gave us eternal encouragement and good hope, [17] encourage your hearts and strengthen you in every good deed and word.

1 Peter 4:8
[8] Above all, love each other deeply, because love covers over a multitude of sins.

Prayer Guide
Our holy, heavenly Father, may your will prevail. Supply our daily needs. Forgive our sins as we forgive others. Protect us from temptation and rescue us from evil. We pray through the name, power and blood of our Lord, Jesus. Amen.

Desire or Dread?

How can we desperately desire and dread the same thing? That is how we often approach our own transition from earthly life to heavenly life. We are so very weary of the burdens of earth and desire the freedom of heaven, yet we cling to our frail human shell with all the tenacity we can muster. The choice is not ours, so we must trust God for the best outcome.

1 Corinthians 15:54-55,57

[54] When the perishable has been clothed with the imperishable, and the mortal with immortality, then the saying that is written will come true: "Death has been swallowed up in victory."

[55] "Where, O death, is your victory?
Where, O death, is your sting?"

[57] But thanks be to God! He gives us the victory through our Lord Jesus Christ.

Prayer Guide
Our holy, heavenly Father, may your will prevail. Supply our daily needs. Forgive our sins as we forgive others. Protect us from temptation and rescue us from evil. We pray through the name, power and blood of our Lord, Jesus. Amen.

Exaggeration

Feelings of inadequacy or attitudes of arrogance are two sides of the coin of exaggeration. Neither is accurate. Those who berate themselves as failures are not perceptive judges, nor are those who overestimate their accomplishments. It would be better if we each ask God to show us how we measure up to his standards.

John 14:23a,24
23a Jesus replied, "Anyone who loves me will obey my teaching. … 24 Anyone who does not love me will not obey my teaching. These words you hear are not my own; they belong to the Father who sent me."

Romans 12:2-3
2 Do not conform to the pattern of this world, but be transformed by the renewing of your mind. Then you will be able to test and approve what God's will is—his good, pleasing and perfect will. 3 For by the grace given me I say to every one of you: Do not think of yourself more highly than you ought, but rather think of yourself with sober judgment, in accordance with the faith God has distributed to each of you.

Philippians 1:9-11
9 And this is my prayer: that your love may abound more and more in knowledge and depth of insight, 10 so that you may be able to discern what is best and may be pure and blameless for the day of Christ, 11 filled with the fruit of righteousness that comes through Jesus Christ—to the glory and praise of God.

Prayer Guide
Our holy, heavenly Father, may your will prevail. Supply our daily needs. Forgive our sins as we forgive others. Protect us from temptation and rescue us from evil. We pray through the name, power and blood of our Lord, Jesus. Amen.

Goals

Our society is goal-oriented—you must have a business plan, profit projections, a vision, a motto. We have sayings such as "If you don't know what you are aiming for, you are sure to hit it." Cute and catchy, but what is the truth? We can make plans and try our hardest and sometimes things just don't work out. A spouse dies or leaves, the market takes a dive, or our own health turns sour. Of course, there is value in looking to the future, but ultimately where should we put our trust?

Proverbs 16:4,8-9

4   The LORD works out everything to its proper end—
       even the wicked for a day of disaster.

8   Better a little with righteousness
       than much gain with injustice.
9   In their hearts humans plan their course,
       but the LORD establishes their steps.

James 4:13-14a,15

[13] Now listen, you who say, "Today or tomorrow we will go to this or that city, spend a year there, carry on business and make money." [14] Why, you do not even know what will happen tomorrow. ... [15] Instead, you ought to say, "If it is the Lord's will, we will live and do this or that."

Prayer Guide

Our holy, heavenly Father, may your will prevail. Supply our daily needs. Forgive our sins as we forgive others. Protect us from temptation and rescue us from evil. We pray through the name, power and blood of our Lord, Jesus. Amen.

It Is God's Will

Often well-meaning people say to those experiencing difficulty, "God is sovereign," "God's got this" or even "It must be God's will." Yes, whatever happens ultimately is God's will. However, there is a vast difference between God's permissive will and his direct or intentional will. God allows (his permissive will) evil, starvation and a multitude of tragedies, which are the end result of man's free will and sin. In the eternal realm, God will bring healing and justice. God's perfect will directs us to be obedient to his word, always to do good and to love as he first loved us.

Genesis 2:16-17
[16] And the Lord God commanded the man, "You are free to eat from any tree in the garden; [17] but you must not eat from the tree of the knowledge of good and evil, for when you eat from it you will certainly die."

Genesis 3:13,17
[13] Then the Lord God said to the woman, "What is this you have done?"
The woman said, "The serpent deceived me, and I ate."
[17] To Adam he said, "Because you listened to your wife and ate fruit from the tree about which I commanded you, 'You must not eat from it,'
"Cursed is the ground because of you;
through painful toil you will eat food from it
all the days of your life."

1 John 4:19,21
[19] We love because he first loved us.
[21] And he has given us this command: Anyone who loves God must also love their brother and sister

---

Prayer Guide
Our holy, heavenly Father, may your will prevail. Supply our daily needs. Forgive our sins as we forgive others. Protect us from temptation and rescue us from evil. We pray through the name, power and blood of our Lord, Jesus. Amen.

Look for Good

Sometimes we have to look for the good because bad is always obvious. God promises that he can bring good out of what seems to be nothing but difficulty. We are responsible to look beyond the surface, realizing that good is not necessarily what we want, nor is it always an easier situation. God's good is from an eternal perspective. Too often people not presently in a tough situation speak in unintentionally hurtful ways, trying to soften our pain by quoting Scriptures or saying after a loved one's death "Well, now she isn't suffering" or "Now she is in a better place." That may be true, but it's insensitive to make such statements when the truth is that we are hurting big time. When on the receiving end of such statements, it's important to reach for God's grace and extend it to those well-meaning but insensitive individuals.

Romans 12:15
[15] Rejoice with those who rejoice; mourn with those who mourn.

Romans 8:28
[28] And we know that in all things God works for the good of those who love him, who have been called according to his purpose.

Philippians 4:8-9
[8] Finally, brothers and sisters, whatever is true, whatever is noble, whatever is right, whatever is pure, whatever is lovely, whatever is admirable—if anything is excellent or praiseworthy—think about such things. [9] Whatever you have learned or received or heard from me, or seen in me—put it into practice. And the God of peace will be with you.

Prayer Guide
Our holy, heavenly Father, may your will prevail. Supply our daily needs. Forgive our sins as we forgive others. Protect us from temptation and rescue us from evil. We pray through the name, power and blood of our Lord, Jesus. Amen.

Need for Peace

When we are distraught, we must realize our greatest needs are met by focusing on God and the answers he provides in the Bible. If we are facing a serious illness or we live with chronic pain, perhaps we ask for healing. Sometimes God grants physical miracles and sometimes he doesn't. The "whys" generally remain unanswered. When the problem is the death or terrible illness of a loved one, the stress on both the suffering one and the caregiver seem almost too much to bear. What is it that we need most to endure and come out victorious? What we need is serenity, or in a straightforward term, PEACE. The answer is within the "Serenity Prayer," which asks God to grant us serenity to accept our circumstances, courage to change them when possible and wisdom to know when we simply have to accept what is happening.

Isaiah 26:3
3   You will keep in perfect peace
      those whose minds are steadfast,
      because they trust in you.

Philippians 4:6-7
[6] Do not be anxious about anything, but in every situation, by prayer and petition, with thanksgiving, present your requests to God. [7] And the peace of God, which transcends all understanding, will guard your hearts and your minds in Christ Jesus.

2 Thessalonians 3:16
[16] Now may the Lord of peace himself give you peace at all times and in every way. The Lord be with all of you.

Prayer Guide
Our holy, heavenly Father, may your will prevail. Supply our daily needs. Forgive our sins as we forgive others. Protect us from temptation and rescue us from evil. We pray through the name, power and blood of our Lord, Jesus. Amen.

Power of Language

It is well-known that positive reinforcement is more effective than criticism. Perhaps we have been the victims of much criticism. Or maybe we are the perpetrators of negativity. Let us choose to practice encouragement so criticism is needed less frequently.

Ephesians 4:29,31-32
[29] Do not let any unwholesome talk come out of your mouths, but only what is helpful for building others up according to their needs, that it may benefit those who listen.

[31] Get rid of all bitterness, rage and anger, brawling and slander, along with every form of malice. [32] Be kind and compassionate to one another, forgiving each other, just as in Christ God forgave you.

Prayer Guide
Our holy, heavenly Father, may your will prevail. Supply our daily needs. Forgive our sins as we forgive others. Protect us from temptation and rescue us from evil. We pray through the name, power and blood of our Lord, Jesus. Amen.

Rehash or Review

We don't take criticism well, especially if we don't think it is valid. We can either rehash what in the moment were hurtful words or review them to determine whether they were merited. It's a difficult task, so we should ask God for insight and direction to show us whether there's any truth or value in the criticism. If God reveals the truth and personal weaknesses or faults are identified, we should now take action to grow as a result. When the criticism is unwarranted or unfair, we need to let it go and forgive.

Proverbs 15:31-33
31 Whoever heeds life-giving correction
　　will be at home among the wise.
32 Those who disregard discipline despise themselves,
　　but the one who heeds correction gains understanding.
33 Wisdom's instruction is to fear the Lord,
　　and humility comes before honor.

Proverbs 17:9
9 Whoever would foster love covers over an offense,
　but whoever repeats the matter separates close friends.

Prayer Guide
Our holy, heavenly Father, may your will prevail. Supply our daily needs. Forgive our sins as we forgive others. Protect us from temptation and rescue us from evil. We pray through the name, power and blood of our Lord, Jesus. Amen.

Self-what?

Society's pendulum swings from one extreme to another. It has gone from self-denial to self-indulgence. In the pursuit of self-assurance, we've over-reacted with self-centeredness. In our focus on self-fulfillment, we've lost the concept of self-discipline. If we want a well-balanced life, we need less emphasis on self and more on God and his principles. Our self-worth must come from being a child of God, adopted by him through Christ's sacrifice. We have been specially chosen through God's gift and our choice of faith to be part of his family.

John 1:12-13
[12] Yet to all who did receive him, to those who believed in his name, he gave the right to become children of God—[13] children born not of natural descent, nor of human decision or a husband's will, but born of God.

Romans 8:14
[14] For those who are led by the Spirit of God are the children of God.

Romans 12:3
[3] For by the grace given me I say to every one of you: Do not think of yourself more highly than you ought, but rather think of yourself with sober judgment, in accordance with the faith God has distributed to each of you.

Prayer Guide
Our holy, heavenly Father, may your will prevail. Supply our daily needs. Forgive our sins as we forgive others. Protect us from temptation and rescue us from evil. We pray through the name, power and blood of our Lord, Jesus. Amen.

The Good Old Days

When things aren't going well, it's common to long for "the good ol' days," but more often than not the good ol' days were not necessarily all that good if we have accurate memories. It's just that the issues that troubled us when we were younger are likely trivial compared to what we now face. Yet comparison in most cases is counterproductive. We cannot recapture what our memories have labeled as "simpler, happier times." Maybe they were, but our need today is to make today a good day, all things considered.

Ecclesiastes 7:9-10

9   Do not be quickly provoked in your spirit,
       for anger resides in the lap of fools.
10   Do not say, "Why were the old days better than these?"
       For it is not wise to ask such questions.

Prayer Guide
Our holy, heavenly Father, may your will prevail. Supply our daily needs. Forgive our sins as we forgive others. Protect us from temptation and rescue us from evil. We pray through the name, power and blood of our Lord, Jesus. Amen.

Tunnel Vision

We have such narrow focus—troubled relationships, physical weaknesses, political problems, financial woes. We don't allow ourselves the broader view of how misunderstandings have been resolved, illnesses endured or healed, the relative unimportance of politics, how our needs have been met to this very day. Since we have survived everything up to this moment, we can trust God to help us see the big picture.

Isaiah 51:5-6
5   My righteousness draws near speedily,
      my salvation is on the way,
      and my arm will bring justice to the nations.
    The islands will look to me
      and wait in hope for my arm.
6   Lift up your eyes to the heavens,
      look at the earth beneath;
    the heavens will vanish like smoke,
      the earth will wear out like a garment
      and its inhabitants die like flies.
    But my salvation will last forever,
      my righteousness will never fail.

Prayer Guide

Our holy, heavenly Father, may your will prevail. Supply our daily needs. Forgive our sins as we forgive others. Protect us from temptation and rescue us from evil. We pray through the name, power and blood of our Lord, Jesus. Amen.

Whose Timing?

Pain ruins our perception of time. It makes the clock slow until we think relief will never come—at least not soon enough. In those instances, we have to reset our clocks to align them with God's time. We need to trust him through everything, knowing whatever happens is in his timing. He will bring true victory. In God's realm there is no more pain.

Psalm 32:3-4

3 When I kept silent,
 my bones wasted away
 through my groaning all day long.
4 For day and night
 your hand was heavy on me;
 my strength was sapped
 as in the heat of summer.

Revelation 21:4

4 "'He will wipe every tear from their eyes. There will be no more death' or mourning or crying or pain, for the old order of things has passed away."

Prayer Guide
Our holy, heavenly Father, may your will prevail. Supply our daily needs. Forgive our sins as we forgive others. Protect us from temptation and rescue us from evil. We pray through the name, power and blood of our Lord, Jesus. Amen.

Chapter 7

Altitude of Attitude 98

Broken Planet 99

Discouraging Words 100

Exasperation 101

God Always Hears. 102

It's You or Me (or Both) 103

Love Is the Key 104

No Looking Back 105

Pray Anyway 106

Religion or Relationship. 107

Shadow Monsters 108

The Higher Goal 109

Unrealistic Expectations 110

Why or How?. 111

Altitude of Attitude

Whether our day is up or down has a lot to do with our focus. When we look up to the Lord, thinking of all he has done for mankind and us personally, life is a lot better than when we look down at our problems and obstacles. It is not simply avoiding the unpleasant; it is looking to God and his word for guidance, whatever the circumstances.

Psalm 91:2,14-16

2   I will say of the Lord, "He is my refuge and my fortress,
    my God, in whom I trust."

14 "Because he loves me," says the Lord, "I will rescue him;
    I will protect him, for he acknowledges my name.
15 He will call on me, and I will answer him;
    I will be with him in trouble,
    I will deliver him and honor him.
16 With long life I will satisfy him
    and show him my salvation."

Ephesians 5:1-2
[1] Follow God's example, therefore, as dearly loved children [2] and walk in the way of love, just as Christ loved us and gave himself up for us as a fragrant offering and sacrifice to God.

Prayer Guide
Our holy, heavenly Father, may your will prevail. Supply our daily needs. Forgive our sins as we forgive others. Protect us from temptation and rescue us from evil. We pray through the name, power and blood of our Lord, Jesus. Amen.

Broken Planet

Hurricanes, tornadoes, forest fires, earthquakes and floods were not part of God's original plan. These natural disasters were not reported from the Garden of Eden. Some scientists think they can explain the "whys," but the core reason is that our habitat as well as our human nature have been off kilter since Adam and Eve first sinned. Humans have done a very poor job of caring for God's creation. Yet to think mankind can fix problems of this magnitude by reducing a carbon footprint is a vast oversimplification. The only power great enough to restore our earth is God Almighty.

Mark 13:8
[8] Nation will rise against nation, and kingdom against kingdom. There will be earthquakes in various places, and famines. These are the beginning of birth pains.

Romans 8:20-22
[20] For the creation was subjected to frustration, not by its own choice, but by the will of the one who subjected it, in hope [21] that the creation itself will be liberated from its bondage to decay and brought into the freedom and glory of the children of God.
[22] We know that the whole creation has been groaning as in the pains of childbirth right up to the present time.

Revelation 21:5
[5] He who was seated on the throne said, "I am making everything new!" Then he said, "Write this down, for these words are trustworthy and true."

Revelation 22:3
[3] No longer will there be any curse. The throne of God and of the Lamb will be in the city, and his servants will serve him.

Prayer Guide
Our holy, heavenly Father, may your will prevail. Supply our daily needs. Forgive our sins as we forgive others. Protect us from temptation and rescue us from evil. We pray through the name, power and blood of our Lord, Jesus. Amen.

Discouraging Words

Sometimes unkind words fly out of our mouths, as if completely bypassing our brains—or at least detouring around discretion. We need to pray that the Holy Spirit will be a filter for our speech. Whether the other party deserves our unbridled harshness is beside the point.

Proverbs 29:20
[20] Do you see someone who speaks in haste?
There is more hope for a fool than for them.

2 Timothy 2:23-24
[23] Don't have anything to do with foolish and stupid arguments, because you know they produce quarrels. [24] And the Lord's servant must not be quarrelsome but must be kind to everyone, able to teach, not resentful.

Prayer Guide
Our holy, heavenly Father, may your will prevail. Supply our daily needs. Forgive our sins as we forgive others. Protect us from temptation and rescue us from evil. We pray through the name, power and blood of our Lord, Jesus. Amen.

Exasperation

When trials and problems hit us one right after another, it feels like the ocean's incessant surf. Another wave pounds us flat just after we have stood up from the last one. In exasperation we may cry out, "What is going on here, God? I don't know what to do or which way to turn. I feel surrounded by defeat! Help me!" This is a common reaction. Keep praying and never give in to negative emotions.

Isaiah 30:19b-21
[19b] How gracious he will be when you cry for help! As soon as he hears, he will answer you. [20] Although the Lord gives you the bread of adversity and the water of affliction, your teachers will be hidden no more; with your own eyes you will see them. [21] Whether you turn to the right or to the left, your ears will hear a voice behind you, saying, "This is the way; walk in it."

Isaiah 33:2
[2] LORD, be gracious to us;
  we long for you.
Be our strength every morning,
  our salvation in time of distress.

Prayer Guide

Our holy, heavenly Father, may your will prevail. Supply our daily needs. Forgive our sins as we forgive others. Protect us from temptation and rescue us from evil. We pray through the name, power and blood of our Lord, Jesus. Amen.

God Always Hears

When we've prayed and God seems not to hear us, his silence does not necessarily mean "No" … it may mean "Wait." If we would add to our prayers "Thy will be done on earth as it is in heaven," we would more clearly understand God's answers, be they "Yes," "No" or "Be patient, my child."

Nehemiah 2:4-5,8b
4 The king said to me, "What is it you want?"
Then I prayed to the God of heaven, 5 and I answered the king, "If it pleases the king and if your servant has found favor in his sight, let him send me to the city in Judah where my ancestors are buried so that I can rebuild it."

8b And because the gracious hand of my God was on me, the king granted my requests.

Matthew 6:10
10   your kingdom come,
     your will be done,
     on earth as it is in heaven.

2 Corinthians 1:20
20 For no matter how many promises God has made, they are "Yes" in Christ. And so through him the "Amen" is spoken by us to the glory of God.

Colossians 1:9
9 For this reason, since the day we heard about you, we have not stopped praying for you. We continually ask God to fill you with the knowledge of his will through all the wisdom and understanding that the Spirit gives,

---

Prayer Guide
Our holy, heavenly Father, may your will prevail. Supply our daily needs. Forgive our sins as we forgive others. Protect us from temptation and rescue us from evil. We pray through the name, power and blood of our Lord, Jesus. Amen.

It's You or Me (or Both)

Current statistics show one in four adults in the United States suffers from depression or anxiety or an even more serious mental illness. That means perhaps everyone reading this has a mental or emotional dysfunction. Therefore, it is probably you and also me! With mental stress and overload so prevalent, what we need is God's love and peace. It is always available. We must accept it as we would any other gift. No gift is helpful unless truly desired.

1 John 4:17-18
[17] This is how love is made complete among us so that we will have confidence on the day of judgment: In this world we are like Jesus. [18] There is no fear in love. But perfect love drives out fear, because fear has to do with punishment. The one who fears is not made perfect in love.

John 14:27
[27] Peace I leave with you; my peace I give you. I do not give to you as the world gives. Do not let your hearts be troubled and do not be afraid.

Prayer Guide
Our holy, heavenly Father, may your will prevail. Supply our daily needs. Forgive our sins as we forgive others. Protect us from temptation and rescue us from evil. We pray through the name, power and blood of our Lord, Jesus. Amen.

Love Is the Key

Whatever the obstacle or the locked door, love is the key. It is the answer to life's questions. Jesus reduced all the law to two concepts: love God first and then your neighbor. From the Old Testament all the way through the Bible, love is taught. We need to put into practice the qualities of love, which are far more than "feel good" emotions. Therefore, learn what the Bible says love is so you can live it through God's strength.

Ephesians 3:14-19
[14] For this reason I kneel before the Father, [15] from whom every family in heaven and on earth derives its name. [16] I pray that out of his glorious riches he may strengthen you with power through his Spirit in your inner being, [17] so that Christ may dwell in your hearts through faith. And I pray that you, being rooted and established in love, [18] may have power, together with all the Lord's holy people, to grasp how wide and long and high and deep is the love of Christ, [19] and to know this love that surpasses knowledge—that you may be filled to the measure of all the fullness of God.

Ephesians 4:2-3
[2] Be completely humble and gentle; be patient, bearing with one another in love. [3] Make every effort to keep the unity of the Spirit through the bond of peace.

Ephesians 5:1-2
[1] Follow God's example, therefore, as dearly loved children [2] and walk in the way of love, just as Christ loved us and gave himself up for us as a fragrant offering and sacrifice to God.

1 Peter 1:22
[22] Now that you have purified yourselves by obeying the truth so that you have sincere love for each other, love one another deeply, from the heart.

Prayer Guide
Our holy, heavenly Father, may your will prevail. Supply our daily needs. Forgive our sins as we forgive others. Protect us from temptation and rescue us from evil. We pray through the name, power and blood of our Lord, Jesus. Amen.

No Looking Back

There is no reverse gear in God's vehicle, so why keep looking at a painful past? It is useful only for learning and letting go. Our only direction should be forward, guided by the ultimate GPS—God, our Personal Savior.

Proverbs 4:11-12
11   I instruct you in the way of wisdom
          and lead you along straight paths.
12   When you walk, your steps will not be hampered;
          when you run, you will not stumble.

Isaiah 43:18
18   "Forget the former things;
          do not dwell on the past."

Prayer Guide
Our holy, heavenly Father, may your will prevail. Supply our daily needs. Forgive our sins as we forgive others. Protect us from temptation and rescue us from evil. We pray through the name, power and blood of our Lord, Jesus. Amen.

Pray Anyway

We pray, but sometimes it is with faith and fear at the same time. We have faith that God can answer our deepest needs, yet we fear that perhaps his answer will not be what we think we need. Pray anyway!

Daniel 3:17-18, 28
[17] "If we are thrown into the blazing furnace, the God we serve is able to deliver us from it, and he will deliver us from Your Majesty's hand. [18] But even if he does not, we want you to know, Your Majesty, that we will not serve your gods or worship the image of gold you have set up."

[28] Then Nebuchadnezzar said, "Praise be to the God of Shadrach, Meshach and Abednego, who has sent his angel and rescued his servants! They trusted in him and defied the king's command and were willing to give up their lives rather than serve or worship any god except their own God."

Acts 20:23-24
[23] I only know that in every city the Holy Spirit warns me that prison and hardships are facing me. [24] However, I consider my life worth nothing to me; my only aim is to finish the race and complete the task the Lord Jesus has given me—the task of testifying to the good news of God's grace.

Prayer Guide
Our holy, heavenly Father, may your will prevail. Supply our daily needs. Forgive our sins as we forgive others. Protect us from temptation and rescue us from evil. We pray through the name, power and blood of our Lord, Jesus. Amen.

Religion or Relationship

"Religion" focuses on our efforts to follow the rules in order to work our way toward God, hoping we've done enough to be accepted. Relationship (with Jesus the Christ) is accepting his love, his light, his constant presence. It is learning the "rules" of Scripture are not punishment but protection … a path to peace and contentment, a life journey with the only true and trustworthy guide.

Matthew 22:37-40
[37] Jesus replied: "'Love the Lord your God with all your heart and with all your soul and with all your mind.' [38] This is the first and greatest commandment. [39] And the second is like it: 'Love your neighbor as yourself.' [40] All the Law and the Prophets hang on these two commandments."

John 6:40
[40] "For my Father's will is that everyone who looks to the Son and believes in him shall have eternal life, and I will raise them up at the last day."

Prayer Guide

Our holy, heavenly Father, may your will prevail. Supply our daily needs. Forgive our sins as we forgive others. Protect us from temptation and rescue us from evil. We pray through the name, power and blood of our Lord, Jesus. Amen.

Shadow Monsters

If we have had a scary, dysfunctional childhood, we may expect monsters in the dark of adulthood. If we have suffered traumatic experiences at any age, we are likely to react to many stimuli with anger, fear or even violence. Psychologists label it PTSD—post-traumatic stress disorder. To get rid of our scary shadows, turn on the light through scriptural truths and/or professional counseling. Those monsters disappear when light is shining.

John 8:12
[12] When Jesus spoke again to the people, he said, "I am the light of the world. Whoever follows me will never walk in darkness, but will have the light of life."

1 Corinthians 13:11
[11] When I was a child, I talked like a child, I thought like a child, I reasoned like a child. When I became a man, I put the ways of childhood behind me.

Prayer Guide
Our holy, heavenly Father, may your will prevail. Supply our daily needs. Forgive our sins as we forgive others. Protect us from temptation and rescue us from evil. We pray through the name, power and blood of our Lord, Jesus. Amen.

The Higher Goal

We spend our energies seeking happiness, when what we need is the joy of the Lord. Happiness is brief and conditional and depends on "happenings." Joy is from the Lord. Joy is knowing the Lord and who he is—the creator and sustainer of everything. If our focus is on the Lord instead of ourselves, then what we gain is eternal. It transcends the best we can know here. It is not a feeling that comes and goes; it is the highest goal of all, knowing Jesus in all his glory.

John 15:10-11
[10] If you keep my commands, you will remain in my love, just as I have kept my Father's commands and remain in his love. [11] I have told you this so that my joy may be in you and that your joy may be complete.

Romans 15:13
[13] May the God of hope fill you with all joy and peace as you trust in him, so that you may overflow with hope by the power of the Holy Spirit.

Prayer Guide
Our holy, heavenly Father, may your will prevail. Supply our daily needs. Forgive our sins as we forgive others. Protect us from temptation and rescue us from evil. We pray through the name, power and blood of our Lord, Jesus. Amen.

Unrealistic Expectations

Many do not want to hear about our troubles, heartaches or pain, even if they care. They literally "wish us well." Seeing our pain makes them uncomfortable and reminds them that they too are vulnerable to distress or disease. To expect others to understand may be unrealistic. If we do have someone who is empathetic, praise God! Yet we must look to our Heavenly Father for lasting solutions.

Psalms 42:11
[11] Why, my soul, are you downcast?
    Why so disturbed within me?
Put your hope in God,
    for I will yet praise him,
    my Savior and my God.

Psalm 50:15
[15] "and call on me in the day of trouble;
    I will deliver you, and you will honor me."

Proverbs 25:20
[20] Like one who takes away a garment on a cold
    or like vinegar poured on a wound,
    is one who sings songs to a heavy heart.

Prayer Guide
Our holy, heavenly Father, may your will prevail. Supply our daily needs. Forgive our sins as we forgive others. Protect us from temptation and rescue us from evil. We pray through the name, power and blood of our Lord, Jesus. Amen.

Why or How?

Probably the biggest question any of us ask God is "Why?" When tragedy strikes or life becomes difficult in any number of ways, we want to place blame. We ask, "Why did God let this happen?" or "Why did God not intervene if he is all powerful?" God seldom explains himself. We can continue to ask unanswerable questions, or we can ask God how to live joyfully in spite of it all. The Old Testament character Job suffered terribly, and his friends implied he must have sinned to be so afflicted. Job complained and questioned, but he did not curse God.

Job 3:25-26
25 "What I feared has come upon me;
    what I dreaded has happened to me.
26 I have no peace, no quietness;
    I have no rest, but only turmoil."

Job 42:12a
12a The LORD blessed the latter part of Job's life more than the former part.

Proverbs 3:5-6
5 Trust in the LORD with all your heart
    and lean not on your own understanding;
6 in all your ways submit to him,
    and he will make your paths straight.

Prayer Guide
Our holy, heavenly Father, may your will prevail. Supply our daily needs. Forgive our sins as we forgive others. Protect us from temptation and rescue us from evil. We pray through the name, power and blood of our Lord, Jesus. Amen.

Chapter 8

Always Pray. 114

Burdens and Loads 115

Distorted Vision 116

Facts and Feeling 117

God Does Provide. 118

Jesus' Touch 119

Love Prays. 120

No More Hope?. 121

Praying Due to Distress. 122

Remember to Remember 123

Sometimes "No" Can Be "Yes" 124

The Worst and the Best. 125

We Can 126

Window or Mirror?. 127

Always Pray

When one's health fails, the possibility of permanent disability looms over us, or the likelihood of our earthly existence soon coming to an end is reality, we should learn to be in constant conversation with God through prayer. There is nothing like total weakness to wake us up. We'd better get to know God on a more intimate level. After all, life on earth is merely the prologue to the reality of life eternal. We should learn to accept God's answers in the perspective of forever.

Luke 18:1
[1] Then Jesus told his disciples a parable to show them that they should always pray and not give up.

Romans 12:12
[12] Be joyful in hope, patient in affliction, faithful in prayer.

Ephesians 6:18
[18] And pray in the Spirit on all occasions with all kinds of prayers and requests. With this in mind, be alert and always keep on praying for all the Lord's people.

Prayer Guide
Our holy, heavenly Father, may your will prevail. Supply our daily needs. Forgive our sins as we forgive others. Protect us from temptation and rescue us from evil. We pray through the name, power and blood of our Lord, Jesus. Amen.

Burdens and Loads

There is a big difference between a burden that is too heavy for any of us to carry alone and the normal workload that we each have responsibility to fulfill. We need to look out for each other and perceive when someone is carrying something that will crush him if he has no help with it. This is the way the Christian family—the church—is supposed to function. We must get to know each other as brothers and sisters—not the quarreling and fighting kind, but those who love and support each other, who come from the same Father and have the same priorities in life. The other type of load is the one that comes from being part of the human race. God created us to work in order to live. The sins of Adam and Eve ruined the ideal Garden of Eden, so we now each have a load to carry.

Matthew 11:28-30
[28] "Come to me, all you who are weary and burdened, and I will give you rest. [29] Take my yoke upon you and learn from me, for I am gentle and humble in heart, and you will find rest for your souls. [30] For my yoke is easy and my burden is light."

Galatians 6:2,4-5
[2] Carry each other's burdens, and in this way you will fulfill the law of Christ.

[4] Each one should test their own actions. Then they can take pride in themselves alone, without comparing themselves to someone else, [5] for each one should carry their own load.

Philippians 2:3b-4
[3b] Rather, in humility value others above yourselves, [4] not looking to your own interests but each of you to the interests of the others.

Prayer Guide
Our holy, heavenly Father, may your will prevail. Supply our daily needs. Forgive our sins as we forgive others. Protect us from temptation and rescue us from evil. We pray through the name, power and blood of our Lord, Jesus. Amen.

Distorted Vision

We wear our negative emotions—loneliness, anger, bitterness, fear, etc.—like glasses with an incorrect prescription. We can see others through them, but there is distortion. It is not an accurate view of what is actually in front of us. To correct this poor focus, we need to get new glasses made according to a Biblical prescription. Know that God never leaves us; let our anger be toward evil, our fear be awe of the Lord.

Isaiah 50:10
10 Who among you fears the LORD
 and obeys the word of his servant?
Let the one who walks in the dark,
 who has no light,
trust in the name of the LORD
 and rely on their God.

Isaiah 51:11
11 Those the LORD has rescued will return.
 They will enter Zion with singing;
 everlasting joy will crown their heads.
Gladness and joy will overtake them,
 and sorrow and sighing will flee away.

Prayer Guide
Our holy, heavenly Father, may your will prevail. Supply our daily needs. Forgive our sins as we forgive others. Protect us from temptation and rescue us from evil. We pray through the name, power and blood of our Lord, Jesus. Amen.

Facts and Feeling

If you have been a Christ-follower for any length of time, you realize there is often a disconnect between who we know the Lord wants us to be (loving, trusting, faithful, confident) and how we feel at an emotional level. We find ourselves either distressed, depressed or downright disgruntled far too often! It is a lifelong battle between our sin nature and our created nature. Despite the certainty of it being an ongoing war this side of Heaven, it is possible, with God's help, to win more battles than not.

1 Corinthians 2:12
[12] What we have received is not the spirit of the world, but the Spirit who is from God, so that we may understand what God has freely given us.

2 Corinthians 10:3-5
[3] For though we live in the world, we do not wage war as the world does. [4] The weapons we fight with are not the weapons of the world. On the contrary, they have divine power to demolish strongholds. [5] We demolish arguments and every pretension that sets itself up against the knowledge of God, and we take captive every thought to make it obedient to Christ.

Prayer Guide
Our holy, heavenly Father, may your will prevail. Supply our daily needs. Forgive our sins as we forgive others. Protect us from temptation and rescue us from evil. We pray through the name, power and blood of our Lord, Jesus. Amen.

God Does Provide

We often cry out to God, reminding him that he has promised to provide for our needs. The problem is what we consider necessary is not always what God defines as essential. Another issue is we do not always recognize provision when God sends it, if it doesn't come in the form we expected. If God's answer or direction seems unclear, look more closely, listen attentively and be willing to wait—for God's timing is often different than what we expect. We do not have an option to define the way God fulfills our needs.

Exodus 16:14-15
[14] When the dew was gone, thin flakes like frost on the ground appeared on the desert floor. [15] When the Israelites saw it, they said to each other, "What is it?" For they did not know what it was.
Moses said to them, "It is the bread the LORD has given you to eat."

Psalm 119:153-154
[153] Look on my suffering and deliver me,
for I have not forgotten your law.
[154] Defend my cause and redeem me;
preserve my life according to your promise.

Prayer Guide
Our holy, heavenly Father, may your will prevail. Supply our daily needs. Forgive our sins as we forgive others. Protect us from temptation and rescue us from evil. We pray through the name, power and blood of our Lord, Jesus. Amen.

Jesus' Touch

Ultimately Jesus' word or touch heals everything. When we look at the magnitude of his life, death and resurrection, we can know all that afflicts us will be resolved. We may struggle, but it is with hope and confidence that maybe here—but definitely in heaven—we will be well.

Matthew 15:30
[30] Great crowds came to him, bringing the lame, the blind, the crippled, the mute and many others, and laid them at his feet; and he healed them.

John 4:47,50
[47] When this man heard that Jesus had arrived in Galilee from Judea, he went to him and begged him to come and heal his son, who was close to death.

[50] "Go," Jesus replied, "your son will live."
The man took Jesus at his word and departed.

Prayer Guide
Our holy, heavenly Father, may your will prevail. Supply our daily needs. Forgive our sins as we forgive others. Protect us from temptation and rescue us from evil. We pray through the name, power and blood of our Lord, Jesus. Amen.

Love Prays

Do not be hesitant to ask for prayer. We all need it. Asking others to pray for us shows our humanity. And praying for someone is the best gift we can give. Love is always willing to pray.

Galatians 6:10
[10] Therefore, as we have opportunity, let us do good to all people, especially to those who belong to the family of believers.

Ephesians 6:18
[18] And pray in the Spirit on all occasions with all kinds of prayers and requests. With this in mind, be alert and always keep on praying for all the Lord's people.

Colossians 4:2
[2] Devote yourselves to prayer, being watchful and thankful.

Prayer Guide
Our holy, heavenly Father, may your will prevail. Supply our daily needs. Forgive our sins as we forgive others. Protect us from temptation and rescue us from evil. We pray through the name, power and blood of our Lord, Jesus. Amen.

No More Hope?

There is no need for hope when we get to heaven, because hope will have been fulfilled by being in God's personal presence. (Yes, God is with us here; but sometimes we deny or doubt since we cannot see him.) While we are still living on earth, hope is essential for our mental health. It is right up there with faith and love. Faith is a decision and a gift from God. It gives us hope, and thus the means to hang on regardless of our circumstances. God's love itself is the source. In sending his only son, Jesus, as a unique sinless sacrifice to pay for our sins, God has made us right for eternity when we accept that wonderful gift. Our faith and hope will be perfectly completed in heaven. Love will last forever.

1 Corinthians 13:13
[13] And now these three remain: faith, hope and love. But the greatest of these is love.

Ephesians 2:8-9
[8] For it is by grace you have been saved, through faith—and this is not from yourselves, it is the gift of God—[9] not by works, so that no one can boast.

1 John 4:7-8,16
[7] Dear friends, let us love one another, for love comes from God. Everyone who loves has been born of God and knows God. [8] Whoever does not love does not know God, because God is love.

[16] And so we know and rely on the love God has for us.
God is love. Whoever lives in love lives in God, and God in them.

Prayer Guide
Our holy, heavenly Father, may your will prevail. Supply our daily needs. Forgive our sins as we forgive others. Protect us from temptation and rescue us from evil. We pray through the name, power and blood of our Lord, Jesus. Amen.

Praying Due to Distress

There are days (even months or years) when we are simply "down and out." Whether the cause is physical, emotional, spiritual or all three, the question remains: "How do I endure?" It is a blessing that the answer is constant: "God will hear and answer our prayers." Sometimes his answer is what we want; other times, not so much. Yet we can be confident that God always hears, and the conclusion of the matter will be for our best eternally.

Psalm 4:1
[1] Answer me when I call to you,
    my righteous God.
Give me relief from my distress;
    have mercy on me and hear my prayer.

Psalm 86:6-7
[6] Hear my prayer, LORD;
    listen to my cry for mercy.
[7] When I am in distress, I call to you,
    because you answer me.

Ecclesiastes 12:13
[13] Now all has been heard;
    here is the conclusion of the matter:
Fear God and keep his commandments,
    for this is the duty of all mankind.

Prayer Guide
Our holy, heavenly Father, may your will prevail. Supply our daily needs. Forgive our sins as we forgive others. Protect us from temptation and rescue us from evil. We pray through the name, power and blood of our Lord, Jesus. Amen.

Remember to Remember

Current crisis or present pain has a way of trumping memory. Take a deep breath and purposely remember. Remember that we have made it through every other life difficulty to this very day. God has been faithful before and always will be. His promises are true regardless of our feelings.

Lamentations 3:49-50,55-57
⁴⁹ My eyes will flow unceasingly,
   without relief,
⁵⁰ until the Lord looks down
   from heaven and sees.

⁵⁵ I called on your name, Lord,
   from the depths of the pit.
⁵⁶ You heard my plea: "Do not close your ears
   to my cry for relief."
⁵⁷ You came near when I called you,
   and you said, "Do not fear."

Romans 8:32
³² He who did not spare his own Son, but gave him up for us all—how will he not also, along with him, graciously give us all things?

Prayer Guide
Our holy, heavenly Father, may your will prevail. Supply our daily needs. Forgive our sins as we forgive others. Protect us from temptation and rescue us from evil. We pray through the name, power and blood of our Lord, Jesus. Amen.

Sometimes "No" Can Be "Yes"

When it seems as if God has answered "No" to our prayers, or all we hear is silence, remember we only see the earthly side of every scene. If we trust that God is good and grants us a heavenly future, we need to realize a "No" down here may be a "Yes" in the bigger eternal picture and to the most important questions. The author of all wisdom knows what is best for us overall.

Psalm 56:3-4
3   When I am afraid, I put my trust in you.
4   In God, whose word I praise—
      in God I trust and am not afraid.
    What can mere mortals do to me?

Psalm 71:20
20   Though you have made me see troubles,
      many and bitter,
      you will restore my life again;
    from the depths of the earth
      you will again bring me up.

Psalm 77:7-8,11-12
7   "Will the Lord reject forever?
      Will he never show his favor again?
8   Has his unfailing love vanished forever?
      Has his promise failed for all time?"

11   "I will remember the deeds of the LORD;
      yes, I will remember your miracles of long ago.
12   I will consider all your works
      and meditate on all your mighty deeds."

Prayer Guide
Our holy, heavenly Father, may your will prevail. Supply our daily needs. Forgive our sins as we forgive others. Protect us from temptation and rescue us from evil. We pray through the name, power and blood of our Lord, Jesus. Amen.

The Worst and the Best

On our worst days—the same as on our best—God is constant, never-changing, always loving and caring. He may or may not make your day better, but his promises never fail. He is with us to the end and beyond.

Psalm 90:15
[15] Make us glad for as many days as you have afflicted us,
for as many years as we have seen trouble.

2 Corinthians 1:20-22
[20] For no matter how many promises God has made, they are "Yes" in Christ. And so through him the "Amen" is spoken by us to the glory of God. [21] Now it is God who makes both us and you stand firm in Christ. He anointed us, [22] set his seal of ownership on us, and put his Spirit in our hearts as a deposit, guaranteeing what is to come.

Prayer Guide
Our holy, heavenly Father, may your will prevail. Supply our daily needs. Forgive our sins as we forgive others. Protect us from temptation and rescue us from evil. We pray through the name, power and blood of our Lord, Jesus. Amen.

We Can

We listen to ourselves more than to anyone else. Too frequently we tell ourselves "I can't" or "Nothing will ever get better." Such negative messages burn themselves into our mental pathways until we take them as fact. With God in our lives, his answer is "Yes, you can!" It is not a godly option to wallow in our mud puddles and declare, "I can't, I'm stuck!" Seek help! Find a Christian community or church which is caring, alive and working together to become more Christlike. Seek those who love and support one another. We cannot do that well unless we try out small groups or classes. An hour on a Sunday morning will not tell you much except whether the pastor is a good speaker or not. Getting to know and support each other within a church or fellowship is vital. We were created to be active participants, not simply passive spectators. Remember, God tells us through it all, "You can!"

Romans 12:2,10-12, 21
2 Do not conform to the pattern of this world, but be transformed by the renewing of your mind. Then you will be able to test and approve what God's will is—his good, pleasing and perfect will.

10 Be devoted to one another in love. Honor one another above yourselves. 11 Never be lacking in zeal, but keep your spiritual fervor, serving the Lord. 12 Be joyful in hope, patient in affliction, faithful in prayer.

21 Do not be overcome by evil, but overcome evil with good.

Philippians 1:9-10
9 And this is my prayer: that your love may abound more and more in knowledge and depth of insight, 10 so that you may be able to discern what is best and may be pure and blameless for the day of Christ,

---

Prayer Guide
Our holy, heavenly Father, may your will prevail. Supply our daily needs. Forgive our sins as we forgive others. Protect us from temptation and rescue us from evil. We pray through the name, power and blood of our Lord, Jesus. Amen.

Window or Mirror?

The function of windows and mirrors can be the basis of an informative analogy. Both are made of glass and allow us to look through or at them. Clear glass windows permit us to see a broad view. They also admit light into dark spaces. Mirrors are glass coated on the back with opaque reflective paint. Clear windows permit us to see "the big picture," while a mirror only shows our own reflections and prevents our view of all that's beyond. When our circumstance is grief (of any sort), it is more constructive to look through a window to a clearer understanding of the possibilities rather than restrict our view to ourselves, which may be distorted if the mirror is held close to our faces.

Isaiah 57:1-2

1 The righteous perish,
   and no one takes it to heart;
  the devout are taken away,
   and no one understands
  that the righteous are taken away
   to be spared from evil.
2 Those who walk uprightly
   enter into peace;
  they find rest as they lie in death.

1 Corinthians 13:12

12 For now we see only a reflection as in a mirror; then we shall see face to face. Now I know in part; then I shall know fully, even as I am fully known.

James 1:23-24

23 Anyone who listens to the word but does not do what it says is like someone who looks at his face in a mirror 24 and, after looking at himself, goes away and immediately forgets what he looks like.

Prayer Guide
Our holy, heavenly Father, may your will prevail. Supply our daily needs. Forgive our sins as we forgive others. Protect us from temptation and rescue us from evil. We pray through the name, power and blood of our Lord, Jesus. Amen.

Chapter 9

Angry?.................................130

Carry On..............................131

Doing the Possible...................132

Familiar Fear.........................133

God Forgives and Forgets.............134

Joy Forever...........................135

Major vs. Minor......................136

Not Alone!............................137

Prepared, Not Petrified..............138

Repetition............................139

Sparrow Prayers......................140

"Thy Will Be Done"..................141

Weakness..............................142

"Woe Is Me" No More.................143

Angry?

When we don't like what is going on in our lives, do we blame God or the devil? Fault really isn't the issue. Believing God is sovereign means he either causes or allows everything. Therefore, even if it seems to be a tragedy for us, it can be used for good by God. Initially we may feel anger toward God, but that is inappropriate if we truly believe he is good all the time. Consider the complete story. Jesus died a cruel death which paid for our salvation. Can we hold on to anger in light of such sacrifice?

Job 40:1-4
1   The Lord said to Job:
2   "Will the one who contends with the Almighty correct him?
     Let him who accuses God answer him!"
3   Then Job answered the Lord:
4   "I am unworthy—how can I reply to you?
     I put my hand over my mouth."

Ephesians 4:31
[31] Get rid of all bitterness, rage and anger, brawling and slander, along with every form of malice.

James 1:19b-20
[19b] Everyone should be quick to listen, slow to speak and slow to become angry, [20] because human anger does not produce the righteousness that God desires.

Prayer Guide
Our holy, heavenly Father, may your will prevail. Supply our daily needs. Forgive our sins as we forgive others. Protect us from temptation and rescue us from evil. We pray through the name, power and blood of our Lord, Jesus. Amen.

Carry On

During World War Two, the British motto was "Keep calm and carry on!" And most of the citizens did just that. We could learn from their determination. We must do our work, care for children, and attend to the elderly or disabled, regardless of our feelings or what is going on in our lives. It is what is right and honorable.

Colossians 3:23-24
[23] Whatever you do, work at it with all your heart, as working for the Lord, not for human masters, [24] since you know that you will receive an inheritance from the Lord as a reward. It is the Lord Christ you are serving.

James 1:27
[27] Religion that God our Father accepts as pure and faultless is this: to look after orphans and widows in their distress and to keep oneself from being polluted by the world.

Prayer Guide
Our holy, heavenly Father, may your will prevail. Supply our daily needs. Forgive our sins as we forgive others. Protect us from temptation and rescue us from evil. We pray through the name, power and blood of our Lord, Jesus. Amen.

Doing the Possible

So often we cannot do much, such as when a friend has a terminal illness or someone special is depressed. Perhaps someone has big debts or loses his/her job. Or maybe you know of a child struggling in school or a single mom who is overwhelmed. These don't even touch on bigger, less personal problems, such as wars, famines and plagues. What shall we do? Pray—and then do what IS possible. Write a note or a card, or text a message of encouragement. Give some money anonymously or get a grocery gift card. Offer to tutor the child or give him an appropriate book. Fix a meal or bake some muffins for the tired mom or an elderly person. Doing just a little often means a lot.

Matthew 10:42
[42] "And if anyone gives even a cup of cold water to one of these little ones who is my disciple, truly I tell you, that person will certainly not lose their reward."

Matthew 25:37,40
[37] "Then the righteous will answer him, 'Lord, when did we see you hungry and feed you, or thirsty and give you something to drink?'"

[40] "The King will reply, 'Truly I tell you, whatever you did for one of the least of these brothers and sisters of mine, you did for me.'"

2 Corinthians 9:12
[12] This service that you perform is not only supplying the needs of the Lord's people but is also overflowing in many expressions of thanks to God.

1 Timothy 6:18
[18] Command them to do good, to be rich in good deeds, and to be generous and willing to share.

Prayer Guide
Our holy, heavenly Father, may your will prevail. Supply our daily needs. Forgive our sins as we forgive others. Protect us from temptation and rescue us from evil. We pray through the name, power and blood of our Lord, Jesus. Amen.

Familiar Fear

Letting go of fears or troubles can be harder than holding on to our known, painful problems. We are so familiar with what is wrong that it becomes easier to live with it than to let go and trust God to carry us through anything—be it life or death.

Psalm 56:3-4
3   When I am afraid, I put my trust in you.
4   In God, whose word I praise—
in God I trust and am not afraid.
What can mere mortals do to me?

Psalm 86:5-7
5   You, Lord, are forgiving and good,
abounding in love to all who call to you.
6   Hear my prayer, LORD;
listen to my cry for mercy.
7   When I am in distress, I call to you,
because you answer me.

Daniel 3:17-18
[17] "If we are thrown into the blazing furnace, the God we serve is able to deliver us from it, and he will deliver us from Your Majesty's hand. [18] But even if he does not, we want you to know, Your Majesty, that we will not serve your gods or worship the image of gold you have set up."

Prayer Guide
Our holy, heavenly Father, may your will prevail. Supply our daily needs. Forgive our sins as we forgive others. Protect us from temptation and rescue us from evil. We pray through the name, power and blood of our Lord, Jesus. Amen.

God Forgives and Forgets

We usually remember our sins and mistakes forever. It is a blessing that God forgives, and then has the ability to forget and erase those wrong actions completely from our records. We'd do well to let them go also, while being grateful that God's love is greater than any of our sins. The only benefit in having memories of words or acts we regret is as a warning not to repeat the sins.

Psalm 103:11-12
11 For as high as the heavens are above the earth,
       so great is his love for those who fear him;
12 as far as the east is from the west,
       so far has he removed our transgressions from us.

Micah 7:19
19 You will again have compassion on us;
       you will tread our sins underfoot
       and hurl all our iniquities into the depths of the sea.

Luke 11:4
4 "'Forgive us our sins,
       for we also forgive everyone who sins against us.
       And lead us not into temptation.'"

Prayer Guide

Our holy, heavenly Father, may your will prevail. Supply our daily needs. Forgive our sins as we forgive others. Protect us from temptation and rescue us from evil. We pray through the name, power and blood of our Lord, Jesus. Amen.

Joy Forever

Being happy is most often a function of circumstance. It happens when things are going well, life is pleasant or we are in the midst of supportive, encouraging people. True joy, by contrast, comes from a deeper source. Joy considers the big picture: the truth of who we are in Christ, how blessed we are by God, and the promises he gives us of life eternal. Happiness is of the here and now. Joy is forever.

Romans 15:13
[13] May the God of hope fill you with all joy and peace as you trust in him, so that you may overflow with hope by the power of the Holy Spirit.

1 Thessalonians 5:16-18
[16] Rejoice always, [17] pray continually, [18] give thanks in all circumstances; for this is God's will for you in Christ Jesus.

Prayer Guide

Our holy, heavenly Father, may your will prevail. Supply our daily needs. Forgive our sins as we forgive others. Protect us from temptation and rescue us from evil. We pray through the name, power and blood of our Lord, Jesus. Amen.

Major vs. Minor

Too often people major in minor issues. They overlook principles and concentrate on particulars. How do others look, or what do they do or say that is at odds with my understanding of an issue? We focus on what divides rather than what unifies. We think "He/she ought..." instead of "How can I show grace?"

Romans 14:13,19
[13] Therefore let us stop passing judgment on one another. Instead, make up your mind not to put any stumbling block or obstacle in the way of a brother or sister.

[19] Let us therefore make every effort to do what leads to peace and to mutual edification.

Romans 15:5-6
[5] May the God who gives endurance and encouragement give you the same attitude of mind toward each other that Christ Jesus had,
[6] so that with one mind and one voice you may glorify the God and Father of our Lord Jesus Christ.

Prayer Guide
Our holy, heavenly Father, may your will prevail. Supply our daily needs. Forgive our sins as we forgive others. Protect us from temptation and rescue us from evil. We pray through the name, power and blood of our Lord, Jesus. Amen.

Not Alone!

We may feel alone, but in fact we are never alone. When feelings threaten to overwhelm you, seek the truth. Scripture tells us repeatedly that God is always with us. He is on our side in all our struggles, directing us in constructive ways. Even though we may lose some battles in life, Jesus Christ has secured our victory in the war.

Psalm 103:13-14

[13] As a father has compassion on his children,
   so the LORD has compassion on those who fear him;
[14] for he knows how we are formed,
   he remembers that we are dust.

Romans 8:33-34

[33] Who will bring any charge against those whom God has chosen? It is God who justifies. [34] Who then is the one who condemns? No one. Christ Jesus who died—more than that, who was raised to life—is at the right hand of God and is also interceding for us.

Prayer Guide

Our holy, heavenly Father, may your will prevail. Supply our daily needs. Forgive our sins as we forgive others. Protect us from temptation and rescue us from evil. We pray through the name, power and blood of our Lord, Jesus. Amen.

Prepared, Not Petrified

Do we do what we do out of fear? Or can we work daily to prepare for any circumstance? If we live in tornado country, it is reasonable to have an emergency kit in a central room or storm cellar. If we reside in the frozen north, it is wise to have warm clothing, food and fuel should the power go off. Panicking over possible—but improbable—emergencies is neither good nor godly. Prepare as best we can, pray and persevere. No crisis lasts forever, but God is eternal. Look to his word for wisdom.

1 Chronicles 29:11-12

11 Yours, Lord, is the greatness and the power
and the glory and the majesty and the splendor,
for everything in heaven and earth is yours.
Yours, Lord, is the kingdom;
you are exalted as head over all.
12 Wealth and honor come from you;
you are the ruler of all things.
In your hands are strength and power
to exalt and give strength to all.

Proverbs 6:6-8

6 Go to the ant, you sluggard;
consider its ways and be wise!
7 It has no commander,
no overseer or ruler,
8 yet it stores its provisions in summer
and gathers its food at harvest.

Matthew 16:2-3

2 He replied, "When evening comes, you say, 'It will be fair weather, for the sky is red,' 3 and in the morning, 'Today it will be stormy, for the sky is red and overcast.' You know how to interpret the appearance of the sky, but you cannot interpret the signs of the times."

Prayer Guide

Our holy, heavenly Father, may your will prevail. Supply our daily needs. Forgive our sins as we forgive others. Protect us from temptation and rescue us from evil. We pray through the name, power and blood of our Lord, Jesus. Amen.

Repetition

Repetition can be good or bad. When the repetition is of a bad habit, it can be destructive. When we allow ourselves continually to have negative reactions to challenges of life, repetition is not constructive. However, when the repetition is of truths we have learned, then it can be comforting. When we remind ourselves of God's faithfulness in the past, it will bring us hope. When we reflect on how God has walked with us or perhaps even carried us through trials and tragedies, we can face the future with courage, knowing He will always be with us through the fire or through the flood.

Psalm 42:5-6a,11

5 Why, my soul, are you downcast?
Why so disturbed within me?
Put your hope in God,
   for I will yet praise him,
   my Savior and my God.
6 My soul is downcast within me;
   therefore I will remember you…

Isaiah 43:2

2 When you pass through the waters,
   I will be with you;
and when you pass through the rivers,
   they will not sweep over you.
When you walk through the fire,
   you will not be burned;
   the flames will not set you ablaze.

Prayer Guide

Our holy, heavenly Father, may your will prevail. Supply our daily needs. Forgive our sins as we forgive others. Protect us from temptation and rescue us from evil. We pray through the name, power and blood of our Lord, Jesus. Amen.

Sparrow Prayers

When we have prayed and prayed about some big issue, illness or crisis in our lives, and we don't think God has paid any attention to our plea, our tendency is to think he does not care. If he doesn't care (our human conclusion), then why bother praying about everyday items. However, we are told many times in Scripture that God does care, he does listen, and he does answer. Sometimes the answer is "No," but we perceive it as silence because we cannot fathom him saying "No" to our heartfelt cry. We must step back and remember God acts in "eternal purpose" mode. There are times when he answers our smallest prayer with a resounding "Yes." This confirms that he does hear and consider every communication from each child of his.

Psalm 138:3
[3] When I called, you answered me;
 you greatly emboldened me.

Matthew 7:11
[11] If you, then, though you are evil, know how to give good gifts to your children, how much more will your Father in heaven give good gifts to those who ask him!

Matthew 10:29-31
[29] Are not two sparrows sold for a penny? Yet not one of them will fall to the ground outside your Father's care. [30] And even the very hairs of your head are all numbered. [31] So don't be afraid; you are worth more than many sparrows.

Prayer Guide
Our holy, heavenly Father, may your will prevail. Supply our daily needs. Forgive our sins as we forgive others. Protect us from temptation and rescue us from evil. We pray through the name, power and blood of our Lord, Jesus. Amen.

"Thy Will Be Done"

To achieve contentment, we must learn to desire God's will more than our own—to consider him highest and holiest of all. We must trust him for our day-to-day needs. We must let go of wrongs done to us, so that we can find the blessed peace of forgiveness. This is God's best for each one of us.

Matthew 6:9-15

9 "This, then, is how you should pray:
"'Our Father in heaven,
hallowed be your name,
10 your kingdom come,
your will be done,
on earth as it is in heaven.
11 Give us today our daily bread.
12 And forgive us our debts,
as we also have forgiven our debtors.
13 And lead us not into temptation,
but deliver us from the evil one.'

14 For if you forgive other people when they sin against you, your heavenly Father will also forgive you. 15 But if you do not forgive others their sins, your Father will not forgive your sins."

Luke 22:42

42 "Father, if you are willing, take this cup from me; yet not my will, but yours be done."

Prayer Guide

Our holy, heavenly Father, may your will prevail. Supply our daily needs. Forgive our sins as we forgive others. Protect us from temptation and rescue us from evil. We pray through the name, power and blood of our Lord, Jesus. Amen.

Weakness

It is not a bad thing to feel weak. Even though the experience is not very pleasant, being fully aware of inadequacy is actually good. For when we know our limitations, our focus is turned toward the only true source of strength—the Lord.

Psalm 16:8
8   I keep my eyes always on the LORD.
     With him at my right hand, I will not be shaken.

Romans 8:26
[26] In the same way, the Spirit helps us in our weakness. We do not know what we ought to pray for, but the Spirit himself intercedes for us through wordless groans.

2 Corinthians 12:10
[10] That is why, for Christ's sake, I delight in weaknesses, in insults, in hardships, in persecutions, in difficulties. For when I am weak, then I am strong.

Prayer Guide
Our holy, heavenly Father, may your will prevail. Supply our daily needs. Forgive our sins as we forgive others. Protect us from temptation and rescue us from evil. We pray through the name, power and blood of our Lord, Jesus. Amen.

"Woe Is Me" No More

So you think you have it worse at this moment than most anyone else? You're experiencing multiple trials: maybe poor health, a loved one dying, not enough money and no prospects of a job that will pay your bills. Your difficulty package is unique. Maybe your problems are worse than many others'. It is not constructive to compare; we must each deal with our own challenges.

John 21:21-22
[21] When Peter saw him, he asked, "Lord, what about him?"
[22] Jesus answered, "If I want him to remain alive until I return, what is that to you? You must follow me."

2 Corinthians 4:8-9,16
[8] We are hard pressed on every side, but not crushed; perplexed, but not in despair; [9] persecuted, but not abandoned; struck down, but not destroyed.

[16] Therefore we do not lose heart. Though outwardly we are wasting away, yet inwardly we are being renewed day by day.

2 Corinthians 6:8-10
[8] through glory and dishonor, bad report and good report; genuine, yet regarded as impostors; [9] known, yet regarded as unknown; dying, and yet we live on; beaten, and yet not killed; [10] sorrowful, yet always rejoicing; poor, yet making many rich; having nothing, and yet possessing everything.

Prayer Guide
Our holy, heavenly Father, may your will prevail. Supply our daily needs. Forgive our sins as we forgive others. Protect us from temptation and rescue us from evil. We pray through the name, power and blood of our Lord, Jesus. Amen.

Chapter 10

Anxious Aging 146

Choose Your Thoughts 147

Don't Compare 148

Fear. 149

God Redeems. 150

Joy, Be Joyful, Rejoice 151

Make Soup 152

One Day at a Time. 153

Principles and Promises 154

Road Rage 155

Standing Firm 156

Timing Is Critical 157

What About Fairness?. 158

Yes and No 159

Anxious Aging

There are many dangers in our world, and it is common to allow our negative imaginations to run wild. Especially as we age and face declining health, it is easy to become anxious. How will I manage? What if I get sick and cannot work? Will I have enough money to last the rest of my life? Will I be able to care for myself? Hasn't God gotten us this far, through good and not so good times? If so, he will see us through the rest of life.

Psalm 121:7-8

7 The LORD will keep you from all harm—
he will watch over your life;
8 the LORD will watch over your coming and going
both now and forevermore.

Isaiah 46:4

4 Even to your old age and gray hairs
I am he, I am he who will sustain you.
I have made you and I will carry you;
I will sustain you and I will rescue you.

Romans 8:37-39

[37] No, in all these things we are more than conquerors through him who loved us. [38] For I am convinced that neither death nor life, neither angels nor demons, neither the present nor the future, nor any powers, [39] neither height nor depth, nor anything else in all creation, will be able to separate us from the love of God that is in Christ Jesus our Lord.

Prayer Guide

Our holy, heavenly Father, may your will prevail. Supply our daily needs. Forgive our sins as we forgive others. Protect us from temptation and rescue us from evil. We pray through the name, power and blood of our Lord, Jesus. Amen.

Choose Your Thoughts

If we could trade places with others once in a while, we would realize everyone has tough times. As it is, we tend to think our problems are the worst. Self-pity is a real poison, while thinking good thoughts can actually cause us to feel better. Let's be intentional and remember some of our enjoyable experiences and visualize beautiful sights we have seen.

Proverbs 14:30
30   A heart at peace gives life to the body,
       but envy rots the bones.

Proverbs 17:22
22   A cheerful heart is good medicine,
       but a crushed spirit dries up the bones.

Colossians 3:2
2 Set your minds on things above, not on earthly things.

Prayer Guide
Our holy, heavenly Father, may your will prevail. Supply our daily needs. Forgive our sins as we forgive others. Protect us from temptation and rescue us from evil. We pray through the name, power and blood of our Lord, Jesus. Amen.

Don't Compare

For the most part, comparisons are counterproductive. Each of us has different skill sets, different opportunities, different obstacles. We have our own battles to fight. That someone else has an easier or harder time is beside the point. While having role models may be positive and inspire us to do better—so far as the person emulates the character of Jesus Christ—the best teacher is Jesus Christ himself. This is another incentive to get to know the Lord through the biblical accounts of his actions and attitudes in all sorts of situations.

John 21:21-22
[21] When Peter saw him, he asked, "Lord, what about him?"
[22] Jesus answered, "If I want him to remain alive until I return, what is that to you? You must follow me."

Hebrews 12:2-3,11
[2] fixing our eyes on Jesus, the pioneer and perfecter of faith. For the joy set before him he endured the cross, scorning its shame, and sat down at the right hand of the throne of God. [3] Consider him who endured such opposition from sinners, so that you will not grow weary and lose heart.

[11] No discipline seems pleasant at the time, but painful. Later on, however, it produces a harvest of righteousness and peace for those who have been trained by it.

Prayer Guide
Our holy, heavenly Father, may your will prevail. Supply our daily needs. Forgive our sins as we forgive others. Protect us from temptation and rescue us from evil. We pray through the name, power and blood of our Lord, Jesus. Amen.

Fear

Fear is the devil's magnifying glass. When we allow fear to consume us, then every possible danger looks more likely and every problem appears even larger than it actually is. Life does have true dangers and many problems, simply because it is earthly and not perfect. Yet approaching life from an attitude of fear distorts and inhibits our abilities to handle the true difficulties we may face. We often get what we expect. If we expect the worst, then our problems will seem much larger than they are. If we decide to make the best of any circumstances, then our problems will be kept in the right perspective and will be easier to overcome.

Joshua 1:9
[9] "Have I not commanded you? Be strong and courageous. Do not be afraid; do not be discouraged, for the LORD your God will be with you wherever you go."

2 Timothy 1:7
[7] For the Spirit God gave us does not make us timid, but gives us power, love and self-discipline.

Prayer Guide
Our holy, heavenly Father, may your will prevail. Supply our daily needs. Forgive our sins as we forgive others. Protect us from temptation and rescue us from evil. We pray through the name, power and blood of our Lord, Jesus. Amen.

God Redeems

There are many sources of sorrow, such as the loss of a loved one; the end of a marriage, relationship or friendship; or even regrets for past mistakes or missed opportunities. We can bear deep wounds from injustices done to us or to certain groups or races. And often our own sins and mistakes can be some of the most difficult wounds to heal. Whatever the cause of our sorrow, our Heavenly Father can redeem the pain, bringing reconciliation to a broken relationship and healing to individual hearts.

Psalm 73:16-17
16 When I tried to understand all this,
     it troubled me deeply
17 till I entered the sanctuary of God;
     then I understood their final destiny.

Psalm 77:11-12
11 "I will remember the deeds of the Lord;
     yes, I will remember your miracles of long ago.
12 I will consider all your works
     and meditate on all your mighty deeds."

Lamentations 3:22,57-58
22 Because of the Lord's great love we are not consumed,
     for his compassions never fail.

57 You came near when I called you,
     and you said, "Do not fear."
58 You, Lord, took up my case;
     you redeemed my life.

Prayer Guide
Our holy, heavenly Father, may your will prevail. Supply our daily needs. Forgive our sins as we forgive others. Protect us from temptation and rescue us from evil. We pray through the name, power and blood of our Lord, Jesus. Amen.

Joy, Be Joyful, Rejoice

The Greek root word CHAIRO is the verb translated into English as "be joyful" in 1 Thessalonians 5:16. There are three other Greek verbs for joy in the Bible. They have other shades of meaning. The idea of CHAIRO is to be joyful or choose joy because we, as Christians, find our joy in God. We have joy in who he is, in what he has done for us and in the eternal hope he has promised us through his son, Jesus Christ. This concept of being joyful is different than being happy. The focus of joy is upward, toward God; the focus of happiness is inward—and dependent on whatever is going on around us. Therefore, we can be unhappy with our circumstances and at the same time have joy in God and in his promises.

1 Thessalonians 5:16a
[16a] Rejoice always, ...

James 1:2-3
[2] Consider it pure joy, my brothers and sisters, whenever you face trials of many kinds, [3] because you know that the testing of your faith produces perseverance.

1 Peter 4:13
[13] But rejoice inasmuch as you participate in the sufferings of Christ, so that you may be overjoyed when his glory is revealed.

Prayer Guide
Our holy, heavenly Father, may your will prevail. Supply our daily needs. Forgive our sins as we forgive others. Protect us from temptation and rescue us from evil. We pray through the name, power and blood of our Lord, Jesus. Amen.

Make Soup

When a friend or loved one is in a tough situation and we are powerless to solve the problem, we can make soup or cookies or buy something at the deli and take the food to the distressed person. (We can even keep some for ourselves!) It will not eliminate the difficulty, but it will make us and our friend feel better. Consider it a prescription of loving kindness. Isn't that what we all need: others to love and care for us?

Mark 8:2-3,8
[2] "I have compassion for these people; they have already been with me three days and have nothing to eat. [3] If I send them home hungry, they will collapse on the way, because some of them have come a long distance."

[8] The people ate and were satisfied. Afterward the disciples picked up seven basketfuls of broken pieces that were left over.

John 13:34
[34] "A new command I give you: Love one another. As I have loved you, so you must love one another."

Galatians 6:2
[2] Carry each other's burdens, and in this way you will fulfill the law of Christ.

Prayer Guide
Our holy, heavenly Father, may your will prevail. Supply our daily needs. Forgive our sins as we forgive others. Protect us from temptation and rescue us from evil. We pray through the name, power and blood of our Lord, Jesus. Amen.

One Day at a Time

When we fret over possible future troubles, we are disregarding God's admonition not to worry. Scripture acknowledges that we will have challenges, but it also tells us to pray about everything and only face one day at a time. We can get through today well with God's help.

Matthew 6:27,31-33
[27] Can any one of you by worrying add a single hour to your life?

[31] So do not worry, saying, 'What shall we eat?' or 'What shall we drink?' or 'What shall we wear?' [32] For the pagans run after all these things, and your heavenly Father knows that you need them. [33] But seek first his kingdom and his righteousness, and all these things will be given to you as well.

Prayer Guide
Our holy, heavenly Father, may your will prevail. Supply our daily needs. Forgive our sins as we forgive others. Protect us from temptation and rescue us from evil. We pray through the name, power and blood of our Lord, Jesus. Amen.

Principles and Promises

The Bible is full of principles and promises. As we read and apply God's word to our individual lives, we should keep in mind what the words or verses say, to whom they were written, and how that Scripture may apply to our own lives at this time. Is it a direction to obey, a principle to observe or a personal promise? What God promises in an eternal sense is not always a "feel good" answer for today. Nevertheless, we must follow God's principles.

Proverbs 4:20-24

[20] My son, pay attention to what I say;
  turn your ear to my words.
[21] Do not let them out of your sight,
  keep them within your heart;
[22] for they are life to those who find them
  and health to one's whole body.
[23] Above all else, guard your heart,
  for everything you do flows from it.
[24] Keep your mouth free of perversity;
  keep corrupt talk far from your lips.

Galatians 3:26-29

[26] So in Christ Jesus you are all children of God through faith, [27] for all of you who were baptized into Christ have clothed yourselves with Christ. [28] There is neither Jew nor Gentile, neither slave nor free, nor is there male and female, for you are all one in Christ Jesus. [29] If you belong to Christ, then you are Abraham's seed, and heirs according to the promise.

Prayer Guide

Our holy, heavenly Father, may your will prevail. Supply our daily needs. Forgive our sins as we forgive others. Protect us from temptation and rescue us from evil. We pray through the name, power and blood of our Lord, Jesus. Amen.

Road Rage

When we cannot control things—such as being stuck behind a large truck in heavy traffic—we can easily become frustrated or angry at a delay or the inability to see ahead. We can take unwise risks trying to pass whatever is blocking our view, or we can choose patience and wait for traffic to start flowing again. The same principle applies to obstacles in our personal life. We would be wise to allow God to make clear the route we need to take. We need God to guide us on the way he knows is best.

Genesis 12:1
[1] The Lord had said to Abram, "Go from your country, your people and your father's household to the land I will show you."

Matthew 2:19-20
[19] After Herod died, an angel of the Lord appeared in a dream to Joseph in Egypt [20] and said, "Get up, take the child and his mother and go to the land of Israel, for those who were trying to take the child's life are dead."

Mark 1:19-20
[19] When he had gone a little farther, he saw James son of Zebedee and his brother John in a boat, preparing their nets. [20] Without delay he called them, and they left their father Zebedee in the boat with the hired men and followed him.

Hebrews 12:1-2a
[1] Therefore, since we are surrounded by such a great cloud of witnesses, let us throw off everything that hinders and the sin that so easily entangles. And let us run with perseverance the race marked out for us, [2a] fixing our eyes on Jesus, the pioneer and perfecter of faith.

Prayer Guide
Our holy, heavenly Father, may your will prevail. Supply our daily needs. Forgive our sins as we forgive others. Protect us from temptation and rescue us from evil. We pray through the name, power and blood of our Lord, Jesus. Amen.

Standing Firm

Who isn't distressed these days? Are the optimists really in denial? Christians are being persecuted around the globe. Children are starving in third-world countries. Our own children dabble in drugs or drop out of school. Disease hits everyone at some point. So where is the good, and how do we stand firm against opposition? God still reigns in the midst of chaos—and it is on that promise we can face the daily battles!

Psalm 93:1
1   The LORD reigns, he is robed in majesty;
     the LORD is robed in majesty and armed with strength;
     indeed, the world is established, firm and secure.

Romans 8:31-32,37
[31] What, then, shall we say in response to these things? If God is for us, who can be against us? [32] He who did not spare his own Son, but gave him up for us all—how will he not also, along with him, graciously give us all things?

[37] No, in all these things we are more than conquerors through him who loved us.

Prayer Guide
Our holy, heavenly Father, may your will prevail. Supply our daily needs. Forgive our sins as we forgive others. Protect us from temptation and rescue us from evil. We pray through the name, power and blood of our Lord, Jesus. Amen.

Timing Is Critical

Waiting feels like wasting time. Yet it is not a waste; lessons take time to learn. God's schedule is always better than ours, even when we do not understand. If we pause to consider past experiences, it can help us be patient as we wait for whatever is to come.

Psalm 107:5-6,8-9
5 They were hungry and thirsty,
   and their lives ebbed away.
6 Then they cried out to the Lord in their trouble,
   and he delivered them from their distress.

8 Let them give thanks to the Lord for his unfailing love
   and his wonderful deeds for mankind,
9 for he satisfies the thirsty
   and fills the hungry with good things.

Lamentations 3:31-32
31 For no one is cast off
   by the Lord forever.
32 Though he brings grief, he will show compassion,
   so great is his unfailing love.

Prayer Guide
Our holy, heavenly Father, may your will prevail. Supply our daily needs. Forgive our sins as we forgive others. Protect us from temptation and rescue us from evil. We pray through the name, power and blood of our Lord, Jesus. Amen.

What About Fairness?

There will always be those who have things better than we do. Yet if we look around, we will realize many in the world live in far worse circumstances than ours. Nowhere in the Bible are we promised a life of ease because we are Christians. We are promised God's presence with us and his justice in eternity.

Psalm 73:3,16-18
3   For I envied the arrogant
      when I saw the prosperity of the wicked.

16 When I tried to understand all this,
      it troubled me deeply
17 till I entered the sanctuary of God;
      then I understood their final destiny.
18 Surely you place them on slippery ground;
      you cast them down to ruin.

Matthew 5:45b
45b He causes his sun to rise on the evil and the good, and sends rain on the righteous and the unrighteous.

Prayer Guide
Our holy, heavenly Father, may your will prevail. Supply our daily needs. Forgive our sins as we forgive others. Protect us from temptation and rescue us from evil. We pray through the name, power and blood of our Lord, Jesus. Amen.

Yes and No

Can we truly understand the supreme "Yes" of Christ's resurrection if we are unwilling to accept God's "No" to our most heartfelt requests and pleadings? The answer is "No." Truly to understand the supreme "Yes" we must have faith. This type of faith is not about the things on earth such as health, wealth and ease of life. This faith is in the eternal hope bought by Christ's crucifixion which was affirmed by his resurrection. Accepting God's "No" without understanding God's reasons is at the core of a faith that knows our eternal hope is a secure "Yes."

Isaiah 55:8
[8] "For my thoughts are not your thoughts,
neither are your ways my ways,"
declares the Lord.

Hebrews 11:1
[1] Now faith is confidence in what we hope for and assurance about what we do not see.

Prayer Guide
Our holy, heavenly Father, may your will prevail. Supply our daily needs. Forgive our sins as we forgive others. Protect us from temptation and rescue us from evil. We pray through the name, power and blood of our Lord, Jesus. Amen.

Chapter 11

Assured Victor 162

Chronic 163

Don't Despair. 164

Emotions vs. Facts 165

His Power 166

Joyful Truth 167

Media Misinformation 168

Overreaction 169

Questions and Answers. 170

Scared Spitless 171

Sufficiency in Weakness 172

To Ruin a Day 173

What Is Enough?. 174

What We Know 175

Assured Victory

To gain victory over opposition we must have faith and declare the truth offered us in the Bible. No one has enough self-generated power; we must draw our strength from God and stand our ground against all evil. Some evil we have allowed to live with us, and some comes from Satan against us. Whatever the source, the solution to getting rid of it is the same: we must cling to our faith, speak biblical truths, resist every evil and trust God's promises for the victory.

James 4:7-8,10
[7] Submit yourselves, then, to God. Resist the devil, and he will flee from you. [8] Come near to God and he will come near to you. Wash your hands, you sinners, and purify your hearts, you double-minded.

[10] Humble yourselves before the Lord, and he will lift you up.

1 Peter 5:8-9
[8] Be alert and of sober mind. Your enemy the devil prowls around like a roaring lion looking for someone to devour. [9] Resist him, standing firm in the faith, because you know that the family of believers throughout the world is undergoing the same kind of sufferings.

Prayer Guide
Our holy, heavenly Father, may your will prevail. Supply our daily needs. Forgive our sins as we forgive others. Protect us from temptation and rescue us from evil. We pray through the name, power and blood of our Lord, Jesus. Amen.

Chronic

Chronic generally implies never ending. It is discouraging to deal with chronic pain, chronic fatigue or any other sort of chronic ailment. On the other hand, God's loving care for us is chronic too, and it will last longer than any of our problems—his love truly is forever.

Psalm 31:9-10
9   Be merciful to me, LORD, for I am in distress;
       my eyes grow weak with sorrow,
       my soul and body with grief.
10   My life is consumed by anguish
       and my years by groaning;
       my strength fails because of my affliction,
       and my bones grow weak.

Psalm 56:13
13   For you have delivered me from death
       and my feet from stumbling,
     that I may walk before God
       in the light of life.

Psalm 57:1
1   Have mercy on me, my God, have mercy on me,
       for in you I take refuge.
     I will take refuge in the shadow of your wings
       until the disaster has passed.

Psalm 63:3
3   Because your love is better than life,
       my lips will glorify you.

Prayer Guide
Our holy, heavenly Father, may your will prevail. Supply our daily needs. Forgive our sins as we forgive others. Protect us from temptation and rescue us from evil. We pray through the name, power and blood of our Lord, Jesus. Amen.

Don't Despair

There are all sorts of reasons we may experience moments of despair. Perhaps a loved one has died or a relationship has dissolved. We may be ill or depressed. Maybe our finances or job situation seem impossible. Whether we allow the circumstances to overwhelm us is our decision. Without minimizing the problems, be encouraged to look beyond them.

1 Peter 5:6,10-11

[6] Humble yourselves, therefore, under God's mighty hand, that he may lift you up in due time.

[10] And the God of all grace, who called you to his eternal glory in Christ, after you have suffered a little while, will himself restore you and make you strong, firm and steadfast. [11] To him be the power for ever and ever. Amen.

Prayer Guide
Our holy, heavenly Father, may your will prevail. Supply our daily needs. Forgive our sins as we forgive others. Protect us from temptation and rescue us from evil. We pray through the name, power and blood of our Lord, Jesus. Amen.

Emotions vs. Facts

When life's road is rough—with multiple detours, accidents, floods or fires—we can be angry and/or doubt God's goodness; we may even start to lose hope. Yet this is the time to believe the facts and not our emotions. The facts are that God's promises are true—in his timing—and that we are never alone. History confirms it, and faith believes it.

Psalm 16:8
8   I keep my eyes always on the LORD.
     With him at my right hand, I will not be shaken.

Psalm 17:6
6   I call on you, my God, for you will answer me;
     turn your ear to me and hear my prayer.

Psalm 18:6,16
6   In my distress I called to the LORD;
     I cried to my God for help.
    From his temple he heard my voice;
     my cry came before him, into his ears.

16   He reached down from on high and took hold of me;
     he drew me out of deep waters.

Psalm 22:4-5
4   In you our ancestors put their trust;
     they trusted and you delivered them.
5   To you they cried out and were saved;
     in you they trusted and were not put to shame.

Prayer Guide

Our holy, heavenly Father, may your will prevail. Supply our daily needs. Forgive our sins as we forgive others. Protect us from temptation and rescue us from evil. We pray through the name, power and blood of our Lord, Jesus. Amen.

His Power

It only takes a moderate crisis to convince us of our weakness. How about a bad migraine or a kidney stone? Consider the implications of a heart attack or a child out of control, or even a crumbling marriage. When any of these obstacles occur in our lives, we quickly realize we have little strength to climb such mountains. The good news is that God does have the power to overcome any roadblock. We metaphorically can enter his elevator and let his power lift us upward, and he will meet us when the doors open. He will be with us and strengthen us, whether the crisis is temporary or terminal.

1 Kings 17:14-16
14 "For this is what the Lord, the God of Israel, says: 'The jar of flour will not be used up and the jug of oil will not run dry until the day the Lord sends rain on the land.'"
15 She went away and did as Elijah had told her. So there was food every day for Elijah and for the woman and her family. 16 For the jar of flour was not used up and the jug of oil did not run dry, in keeping with the word of the Lord spoken by Elijah.

2 Corinthians 12:8-10
8 Three times I pleaded with the Lord to take it away from me. 9 But he said to me, "My grace is sufficient for you, for my power is made perfect in weakness." Therefore I will boast all the more gladly about my weaknesses, so that Christ's power may rest on me. 10 That is why, for Christ's sake, I delight in weaknesses, in insults, in hardships, in persecutions, in difficulties. For when I am weak, then I am strong.

2 Corinthians 13:4
4 For to be sure, he was crucified in weakness, yet he lives by God's power. Likewise, we are weak in him, yet by God's power we will live with him in our dealing with you.

Prayer Guide
Our holy, heavenly Father, may your will prevail. Supply our daily needs. Forgive our sins as we forgive others. Protect us from temptation and rescue us from evil. We pray through the name, power and blood of our Lord, Jesus. Amen.

Joyful Truth

One of the evil one's biggest lies is that we must attain some level of goodness to earn our way to heaven. Not true! God's greatest gift to us is unconditional love: the life and death of his Son, Jesus Christ, paying the price to atone for all our sins. Jesus' resurrection assures our future life after sin and death—the truth of heaven!

Psalm 145:9
[9] The Lord is good to all;
    he has compassion on all he has made.

Romans 5:6
[6] You see, at just the right time, when we were still powerless, Christ died for the ungodly.

Ephesians 2:4-5
[4] But because of his great love for us, God, who is rich in mercy, [5] made us alive with Christ even when we were dead in transgressions—it is by grace you have been saved.

Prayer Guide
Our holy, heavenly Father, may your will prevail. Supply our daily needs. Forgive our sins as we forgive others. Protect us from temptation and rescue us from evil. We pray through the name, power and blood of our Lord, Jesus. Amen.

Media Misinformation

When everything wrong or ugly is all we see and hear, it is discouraging. It also skews our perceptions about life. We gain from less exposure to opinion and more focus on God and good. Turn off the TV and computer, and stop scanning your phone every other minute. Go for a walk in nature or look at photos of stunning scenery. Let creation speak of the creator.

Psalm 27:13-14

[13] I remain confident of this:
I will see the goodness of the LORD
in the land of the living.
[14] Wait for the LORD;
be strong and take heart
and wait for the LORD.

Psalm 121:1-2

[1] I lift up my eyes to the mountains—
where does my help come from?
[2] My help comes from the LORD,
the Maker of heaven and earth.

Romans 1:20

[20] For since the creation of the world God's invisible qualities—his eternal power and divine nature—have been clearly seen, being understood from what has been made, so that people are without excuse.

Prayer Guide

Our holy, heavenly Father, may your will prevail. Supply our daily needs. Forgive our sins as we forgive others. Protect us from temptation and rescue us from evil. We pray through the name, power and blood of our Lord, Jesus. Amen.

Overreaction

We often have extreme reactions. We get sick or experience difficult pain and we're either afraid we will die or—when truly miserable—we wish we would leave this body right now! We don't want to call trials joy, nor do we really want to learn perseverance. However, if that is God's lesson plan for this time, then we need to heed it.

Psalm 4:1
1   Answer me when I call to you,
      my righteous God.
    Give me relief from my distress;
      have mercy on me and hear my prayer.

Isaiah 55:8-9
8   "For my thoughts are not your thoughts,
      neither are your ways my ways,"
    declares the LORD.
9   "As the heavens are higher than the earth,
      so are my ways higher than your ways
      and my thoughts than your thoughts."

James 1:2-4
2 Consider it pure joy, my brothers and sisters, whenever you face trials of many kinds, 3 because you know that the testing of your faith produces perseverance. 4 Let perseverance finish its work so that you may be mature and complete, not lacking anything.

Prayer Guide
Our holy, heavenly Father, may your will prevail. Supply our daily needs. Forgive our sins as we forgive others. Protect us from temptation and rescue us from evil. We pray through the name, power and blood of our Lord, Jesus. Amen.

Questions and Answers

Do we camp out in the questions of life, wallowing in the "What ifs?" Or can we change, living most of our days in the beauty of the answers we do have? Let our focus be less on the problems and more on the solutions; not so much on a far-off future as on the small joys of the journey.

Luke 12:29-31
[29] And do not set your heart on what you will eat or drink; do not worry about it. [30] For the pagan world runs after all such things, and your Father knows that you need them. [31] But seek his kingdom, and these things will be given to you as well.

Romans 6:22
[22] But now that you have been set free from sin and have become slaves of God, the benefit you reap leads to holiness, and the result is eternal life.

Philippians 4:4
[4] Rejoice in the Lord always. I will say it again: Rejoice!

Prayer Guide
Our holy, heavenly Father, may your will prevail. Supply our daily needs. Forgive our sins as we forgive others. Protect us from temptation and rescue us from evil. We pray through the name, power and blood of our Lord, Jesus. Amen.

Scared Spitless

At some point we all go through heart-wrenching or terrifying times that "scare us spitless." A woman finds a lump that was not there last month. An employee is fired with no warning. One opens the front door to a pastor or policeman who says the heart-stopping words, "There has been a terrible wreck, and I'm so sorry, your child/spouse/parent did not survive." Whatever the circumstance, we Christians must find our strength in God. And it's better to realize he is our source before the moment we realize we have no strength of our own.

Joshua 1:9
9 "Have I not commanded you? Be strong and courageous. Do not be afraid; do not be discouraged, for the LORD your God will be with you wherever you go."

Psalm 55:4-5,16
4   My heart is in anguish within me;
         the terrors of death have fallen on me.
5   Fear and trembling have beset me;
         horror has overwhelmed me.

16   As for me, I call to God,
         and the LORD saves me.

Psalm 56:3,11
3   When I am afraid, I put my trust in you.

11   in God I trust and am not afraid.
         What can man do to me?

Romans 8:37
37 No, in all these things we are more than conquerors through him who loved us

---

Prayer Guide
Our holy, heavenly Father, may your will prevail. Supply our daily needs. Forgive our sins as we forgive others. Protect us from temptation and rescue us from evil. We pray through the name, power and blood of our Lord, Jesus. Amen.

Sufficiency in Weakness

Whether our battle is disease, divorce, death or plain old discouragement, God's word has antidotes for every poisonous dose from the devil. When we realize our weaknesses and need for God's strength, then we are on the right track.

Job 42:1-3,10
[1] Then Job replied to the LORD:
[2] "I know that you can do all things;
no purpose of yours can be thwarted.
[3] You asked, 'Who is this that obscures my plans without knowledge?'
Surely I spoke of things I did not understand,
things too wonderful for me to know."

[10] After Job had prayed for his friends, the LORD restored his fortunes and gave him twice as much as he had before.

2 Corinthians 12:7b-10
[7b] Therefore, in order to keep me from becoming conceited, I was given a thorn in my flesh, a messenger of Satan, to torment me. [8] Three times I pleaded with the Lord to take it away from me. [9] But he said to me, "My grace is sufficient for you, for my power is made perfect in weakness." Therefore I will boast all the more gladly about my weaknesses, so that Christ's power may rest on me. [10] That is why, for Christ's sake, I delight in weaknesses, in insults, in hardships, in persecutions, in difficulties. For when I am weak, then I am strong.

Prayer Guide
Our holy, heavenly Father, may your will prevail. Supply our daily needs. Forgive our sins as we forgive others. Protect us from temptation and rescue us from evil. We pray through the name, power and blood of our Lord, Jesus. Amen.

To Ruin a Day

There are two sure ways to upset ourselves and ruin our day. One is to dwell on past problems, and the other is to worry about the future. Neither thought pattern changes anything for the better. Be reminded to focus on the tasks of today and the promises of God.

Matthew 6:34
[34] Therefore do not worry about tomorrow, for tomorrow will worry about itself. Each day has enough trouble of its own.

Romans 6:14
[14] For sin shall no longer be your master, because you are not under the law, but under grace.

Hebrews 3:15
[15] As has just been said:
> "Today, if you hear his voice,
> do not harden your hearts
> as you did in the rebellion."

Hebrews 4:16
[16] Let us then approach God's throne of grace with confidence, so that we may receive mercy and find grace to help us in our time of need.

Prayer Guide
Our holy, heavenly Father, may your will prevail. Supply our daily needs. Forgive our sins as we forgive others. Protect us from temptation and rescue us from evil. We pray through the name, power and blood of our Lord, Jesus. Amen.

What Is Enough?

When we think we can never be good enough to live life successfully, much less get into heaven, we are right! We all make so many mistakes, but only our rejection of Jesus Christ can defeat us. What to do? Understand that in Jesus, through his sacrifice on the cross, we can manage life day by day. We are unable to be good enough or do enough to earn a ticket to heaven; but Jesus was sinless and did it for us. In the end, his love is enough.

Matthew 10:32-33
[32] "Whoever acknowledges me before others, I will also acknowledge before my Father in heaven. [33] But whoever disowns me before others, I will disown before my Father in heaven."

Romans 3:22-24
[22] This righteousness is given through faith in Jesus Christ to all who believe. There is no difference between Jew and Gentile, [23] for all have sinned and fall short of the glory of God, [24] and all are justified freely by his grace through the redemption that came by Christ Jesus.

Romans 8:3-4
[3] For what the law was powerless to do because it was weakened by the flesh, God did by sending his own Son in the likeness of sinful flesh to be a sin offering. And so he condemned sin in the flesh, [4] in order that the righteous requirement of the law might be fully met in us, who do not live according to the flesh but according to the Spirit.

Prayer Guide
Our holy, heavenly Father, may your will prevail. Supply our daily needs. Forgive our sins as we forgive others. Protect us from temptation and rescue us from evil. We pray through the name, power and blood of our Lord, Jesus. Amen.

What We Know

It is not how we feel but what we know! Emotions are unreliable indicators. So many factors influence how we feel—everything from chronic pain to hormones to brain chemical imbalances, not to mention daily life difficulties. When we feel down or discouraged, we should review and remember the truths that are recorded over and over in God's word.

John 8:31-32,36
[31] To the Jews who had believed him, Jesus said, "If you hold to my teaching, you are really my disciples. [32] Then you will know the truth, and the truth will set you free."

[36] So if the Son sets you free, you will be free indeed.

2 Timothy 3:16-17
[16] All Scripture is God-breathed and is useful for teaching, rebuking, correcting and training in righteousness, [17] so that the servant of God may be thoroughly equipped for every good work.

Hebrews 4:12
[12] For the word of God is alive and active. Sharper than any double-edged sword, it penetrates even to dividing soul and spirit, joints and marrow; it judges the thoughts and attitudes of the heart.

Prayer Guide
Our holy, heavenly Father, may your will prevail. Supply our daily needs. Forgive our sins as we forgive others. Protect us from temptation and rescue us from evil. We pray through the name, power and blood of our Lord, Jesus. Amen.

Chapter 12

Bad News, Good News 178

Clichés. 179

Each One Help One 180

First Things First 181

How to Wait. 182

Know Your Enemy. 183

Look to the Light 184

Overwhelmed 185

Questions, Questions 186

Seasons of Struggle 187

Take Your Medicine. 188

To Sleep or Not 189

What Is, Not "What If?" 190

The Final Focus. 191

Bad News, Good News

The bad news: We sin every day because we fall short of God's standards in many ways, be it through deeds or words. The good news: Jesus' death paid the price for each one who is willing to believe and accept that priceless gift. His resurrection assures us of the very good news that we too will live again.

Romans 3:10,12b
[10] As it is written:
> "There is no one righteous, not even one;
> there is no one who understands;
> there is no one who seeks God.

[12b] "... there is no one who does good,
not even one."

Romans 5:6
[6] You see, at just the right time, when we were still powerless, Christ died for the ungodly.

Romans 6:4-5
[4] We were therefore buried with him through baptism into death in order that, just as Christ was raised from the dead through the glory of the Father, we too may live a new life.
[5] For if we have been united with him in a death like his, we will certainly also be united with him in a resurrection like his.

Prayer Guide
Our holy, heavenly Father, may your will prevail. Supply our daily needs. Forgive our sins as we forgive others. Protect us from temptation and rescue us from evil. We pray through the name, power and blood of our Lord, Jesus. Amen.

Clichés

Every culture has its clichés. These phrases have been repeated so often they almost sound like the gospel truth. Unfortunately, while they have perhaps a grain of truth in them, they actually can lead us to mistaken conclusions. Sayings such as "If you can't do it well, then don't do it at all" can lead to unhealthy perfectionism. Another cliché is "Practice makes perfect!" Practice may improve performance, but it doesn't make us perfect. We need to accept our humanity, our lack of perfection outside of Christ Jesus. We have a spiritual obligation to be his good representatives. We also need to develop a realistic expectation of life–it is not going to be fair. Remember, people are not necessarily how they appear on social media. They may or may not be fulfilling their true potential. Our responsibility is to use what talents God has given us to the best of our ability.

Psalm 73:3,16-17

3   For I envied the arrogant
      when I saw the prosperity of the wicked.

16   When I tried to understand all this,
      it troubled me deeply
17   till I entered the sanctuary of God;
      then I understood their final destiny.

Colossians 3:23-24

23 Whatever you do, work at it with all your heart, as working for the Lord, not for human masters, 24 since you know that you will receive an inheritance from the Lord as a reward. It is the Lord Christ you are serving.

Prayer Guide
Our holy, heavenly Father, may your will prevail. Supply our daily needs. Forgive our sins as we forgive others. Protect us from temptation and rescue us from evil. We pray through the name, power and blood of our Lord, Jesus. Amen.

Each One Help One

Each of us has struggles. There are relatively minor ones such as hurtful words, a flat tire or constant conflicts with associates. There are major issues like adultery, domestic abuse, loss of a job, deception and lies within families. There are global threats from political or sectarian crises; not to mention natural disasters of every sort. Millions of lives are affected year after year. Our world is broken on so many levels. What can we do? We can pray, encourage and help one person every day. Even seemingly small acts of compassion truly can make a difference for those on the receiving end.

Matthew 10:42
[42] "And if anyone gives even a cup of cold water to one of these little ones who is my disciple, truly I tell you, that person will certainly not lose their reward."

Matthew 25:40
[40] "The King will reply, 'Truly I tell you, whatever you did for one of the least of these brothers and sisters of mine, you did for me.'"

Ephesians 4:29
[29] Do not let any unwholesome talk come out of your mouths, but only what is helpful for building others up according to their needs, that it may benefit those who listen.

Ephesians 6:18
[18] And pray in the Spirit on all occasions with all kinds of prayers and requests. With this in mind, be alert and always keep on praying for all the Lord's people.

Prayer Guide
Our holy, heavenly Father, may your will prevail. Supply our daily needs. Forgive our sins as we forgive others. Protect us from temptation and rescue us from evil. We pray through the name, power and blood of our Lord, Jesus. Amen.

First Things First

We have to stay and be before we can go and do. If a flowering plant is cut off from its root, the nourishment no longer flows throughout the plant; it cannot continue to grow. While a cut bouquet may look pretty for a few days, it will not reproduce or even open new buds for very long. We too must stay attached to our vine in order to live and produce new fruit.

John 15:4-6
[4] Remain in me, as I also remain in you. No branch can bear fruit by itself; it must remain in the vine. Neither can you bear fruit unless you remain in me.
[5] "I am the vine; you are the branches. If you remain in me and I in you, you will bear much fruit; apart from me you can do nothing. 6 If you do not remain in me, you are like a branch that is thrown away and withers; such branches are picked up, thrown into the fire and burned."

Romans 11:17-18
[17] If some of the branches have been broken off, and you, though a wild olive shoot, have been grafted in among the others and now share in the nourishing sap from the olive root, [18] do not consider yourself to be superior to those other branches. If you do, consider this: You do not support the root, but the root supports you.

Prayer Guide
Our holy, heavenly Father, may your will prevail. Supply our daily needs. Forgive our sins as we forgive others. Protect us from temptation and rescue us from evil. We pray through the name, power and blood of our Lord, Jesus. Amen.

How to Wait

One of life's more difficult challenges is waiting: waiting for healing, waiting for restoration, waiting for answers or understanding. It increases the burden if the challenge was someone else's fault. That presents the need for forgiveness. It is one thing when a challenge is due to an accident, and more frustrating when someone's negligence was the cause; but it's terribly hard if the harm was intentional. Still, the Bible admonishes us to persevere and follow Christ's example.

Romans 8:25-26
[25] But if we hope for what we do not yet have, we wait for it patiently. [26] In the same way, the Spirit helps us in our weakness. We do not know what we ought to pray for, but the Spirit himself intercedes for us through wordless groans.

2 Thessalonians 3:5
[5] May the Lord direct your hearts into God's love and Christ's perseverance.

James 1:3-4,12
[3] because you know that the testing of your faith produces perseverance. [4] Let perseverance finish its work so that you may be mature and complete, not lacking anything.

[12] Blessed is the one who perseveres under trial because, having stood the test, that person will receive the crown of life that the Lord has promised to those who love him.

James 5:10-11
[10] Brothers and sisters, as an example of patience in the face of suffering, take the prophets who spoke in the name of the Lord. [11] As you know, we count as blessed those who have persevered. You have heard of Job's perseverance and have seen what the Lord finally brought about. The Lord is full of compassion and mercy.

Prayer Guide
Our holy, heavenly Father, may your will prevail. Supply our daily needs. Forgive our sins as we forgive others. Protect us from temptation and rescue us from evil. We pray through the name, power and blood of our Lord, Jesus. Amen.

Know Your Enemy

Satan is our biggest enemy—and by following his deceiving ways (whether we are tricked or do so intentionally), we are always in danger. We speak before we think and act to benefit ourselves. Maturing in Christian behavior requires wise choices, self-denial and conscious work. We acknowledge salvation comes only through God's grace. This does not mean life will become easier; if anything, it often becomes harder once we are aware of what is good and what is not.

Ephesians 2:8-10
[8] For it is by grace you have been saved, through faith—and this is not from yourselves, it is the gift of God—[9] not by works, so that no one can boast. [10] For we are God's handiwork, created in Christ Jesus to do good works, which God prepared in advance for us to do.

James 3:13-16
[13] Who is wise and understanding among you? Let them show it by their good life, by deeds done in the humility that comes from wisdom. [14] But if you harbor bitter envy and selfish ambition in your hearts, do not boast about it or deny the truth. [15] Such "wisdom" does not come down from heaven but is earthly, unspiritual, demonic. [16] For where you have envy and selfish ambition, there you find disorder and every evil practice.

James 4:1-3
[1] What causes fights and quarrels among you? Don't they come from your desires that battle within you? [2] You desire but do not have, so you kill. You covet but you cannot get what you want, so you quarrel and fight. You do not have because you do not ask God. [3] When you ask, you do not receive, because you ask with wrong motives, that you may spend what you get on your pleasures.

Prayer Guide

Our holy, heavenly Father, may your will prevail. Supply our daily needs. Forgive our sins as we forgive others. Protect us from temptation and rescue us from evil. We pray through the name, power and blood of our Lord, Jesus. Amen.

Look to the Light

People in distress spend a lot of time looking in the mirror. They reflect their own problems instead of looking at the stars. Better yet, we should focus on the Star of Bethlehem, which is a symbol directing attention to the child Jesus, born in a stable two thousand years ago, who was and is the "Light of the World." We don't learn much looking at ourselves all the time. The light of the Lord brings understanding and hope.

Psalm 50:15
15 "and call on me in the day of trouble;
I will deliver you, and you will honor me."

Matthew 2:2
2 ..."Where is the one who has been born king of the Jews? We saw his star when it rose and have come to worship him."

John 1:3-4,9
3 Through him all things were made; without him nothing was made that has been made. 4 In him was life, and that life was the light of all mankind.

9 The true light that gives light to everyone was coming into the world.

Prayer Guide
Our holy, heavenly Father, may your will prevail. Supply our daily needs. Forgive our sins as we forgive others. Protect us from temptation and rescue us from evil. We pray through the name, power and blood of our Lord, Jesus. Amen.

Overwhelmed

We've prayed the "Serenity Prayer" so many times that we think we have learned to accept, to act and to discern. Then something else happens: a bad medical report, a financial crisis, a loved one in trouble. Or perhaps two or more difficulties strike at once. We can become overwhelmed. What shall we do? Pray, ask others to pray, trust God and wait...not an easy assignment, but well worth the effort.

2 Chronicles 20:12b,15b,17
[12b] "We do not know what to do, but our eyes are on you."

[15b] [Jahaziel, son of Zechariah] said: "This is what the Lord says to you: 'Do not be afraid or discouraged because of this vast army. For the battle is not yours, but God's. ... [17] You will not have to fight this battle. Take up your positions; stand firm and see the deliverance the Lord will give you, Judah and Jerusalem. Do not be afraid; do not be discouraged. Go out to face them tomorrow, and the Lord will be with you.'"

Ephesians 6:10,12
[10] Finally, be strong in the Lord and in his mighty power.

[12] For our struggle is not against flesh and blood, but against the rulers, against the authorities, against the powers of this dark world and against the spiritual forces of evil in the heavenly realms.

Colossians 4:2
[2] Devote yourselves to prayer, being watchful and thankful.

James 5:16
[16] Therefore confess your sins to each other and pray for each other so that you may be healed. The prayer of a righteous person is powerful and effective

---

Prayer Guide
Our holy, heavenly Father, may your will prevail. Supply our daily needs. Forgive our sins as we forgive others. Protect us from temptation and rescue us from evil. We pray through the name, power and blood of our Lord, Jesus. Amen.

Questions, Questions

We so often ask "Why?" and "When?"—but better questions are "Who?" and "How?" "Why" something happened does not change anything. "When" is seldom answered. But "Who" is our strength and "How" we can live by God's guidelines are always important.

Psalm 94:18-19
18   When I said, "My foot is slipping,"
        your unfailing love, LORD, supported me.
19   When anxiety was great within me,
        your consolation brought me joy.

Ephesians 5:15-16
[15] Be very careful, then, how you live—not as unwise but as wise,
[16] making the most of every opportunity, because the days are evil.

Prayer Guide
Our holy, heavenly Father, may your will prevail. Supply our daily needs. Forgive our sins as we forgive others. Protect us from temptation and rescue us from evil. We pray through the name, power and blood of our Lord, Jesus. Amen.

Seasons of Struggle

True optimists are a minority. And persistent pessimists are not a majority. While some people have actual clinical depression needing medication and counseling, most of us are in the middle, going through seasons of struggle and good times. Even strong, famous men in history have wrestled with the black dog of depression. Consider Israel's King David, Elijah, Jeremiah (often called the weeping prophet) and Job. American President Abraham Lincoln and British Prime Minister Winston Churchill suffered with bouts of darkness. Lincoln said he went to his knees because he did not know anywhere else to go. Churchill retreated to paint away his woes. We all must learn how to deal with situational depression because hard times are hard! To solve our depression in healthy ways (not using drugs, alcohol or isolation), we must first cry out in heartfelt prayer to God, and then we must seek help from our church family.

1 Kings 19:3-6
3 Elijah was afraid and ran for his life. When he came to Beersheba in Judah, he left his servant there, 4 while he himself went a day's journey into the wilderness. He came to a broom bush, sat down under it and prayed that he might die. "I have had enough, Lord," he said. "Take my life; I am no better than my ancestors." 5 Then he lay down under the bush and fell asleep.
All at once an angel touched him and said, "Get up and eat." 6 He looked around, and there by his head was some bread baked over hot coals, and a jar of water. He ate and drank and then lay down again.

Psalm 57:1
1   Have mercy on me, my God, have mercy on me,
      for in you I take refuge.
    I will take refuge in the shadow of your wings
      until the disaster has passed.

Prayer Guide
Our holy, heavenly Father, may your will prevail. Supply our daily needs. Forgive our sins as we forgive others. Protect us from temptation and rescue us from evil. We pray through the name, power and blood of our Lord, Jesus. Amen.

Take Your Medicine!

We can be such stubborn people! Something is hurting and we have some medicine that has the potential to help. Do we take it knowing the risks involved and get better, being able to function again? No, we procrastinate, or we say, "Well, maybe this will get better on its own." Or possibly, "I think I'll wait until it gets worse before I take any medicine." We need to realize that if the pain is enough to interrupt our lives then we need to take the medicine! The Lord has given skills to medical people and to counselors so they can help others, whether the pain is physical or emotional. It is a gift given to provide relief. We need to take the medicine and say, "Thank You, Lord, that you provided help in this way."

2 Kings 5:13-14
[13] Naaman's servants went to him and said, "My father, if the prophet had told you to do some great thing, would you not have done it? How much more, then, when he tells you, 'Wash and be cleansed'!" [14] So he went down and dipped himself in the Jordan seven times, as the man of God had told him, and his flesh was restored and became clean like that of a young boy.

Isaiah 38:21
[21] Isaiah had said, "Prepare a poultice of figs and apply it to the boil, and he will recover."

Luke 10:34
[34] He went to him and bandaged his wounds, pouring on oil and wine. Then he put the man on his own donkey, brought him to an inn and took care of him.

Prayer Guide
Our holy, heavenly Father, may your will prevail. Supply our daily needs. Forgive our sins as we forgive others. Protect us from temptation and rescue us from evil. We pray through the name, power and blood of our Lord, Jesus. Amen.

To Sleep or Not

Sleep can be restorative when the body is tired, ill or stressed. However, excessive sleep can be an escape mechanism and/or a symptom of depression. Various factors, such as physical aging, can disrupt good sleep habits. We have some control over our patterns of rest and benefit if we establish healthy practices. It helps to turn off electronics a couple of hours before bedtime and go to bed and arise at regular times. Should we need professional help—medical or emotional—we would be wise to seek it promptly. Enough sleep, but not too much, is what we need.

Psalm127:2
2 In vain you rise early
    and stay up late,
   toiling for food to eat—
    for he grants sleep to those he loves.

Proverbs 3:24
24 When you lie down, you will not be afraid;
    when you lie down, your sleep will be sweet.

Proverbs 6:9-11
9 How long will you lie there, you sluggard?
    When will you get up from your sleep?
10 A little sleep, a little slumber,
    a little folding of the hands to rest—
11 and poverty will come on you like a thief
    and scarcity like an armed man.

Proverbs 19:15
15 Laziness brings on deep sleep,
    and the shiftless go hungry.

Prayer Guide
Our holy, heavenly Father, may your will prevail. Supply our daily needs. Forgive our sins as we forgive others. Protect us from temptation and rescue us from evil. We pray through the name, power and blood of our Lord, Jesus. Amen.

What Is, Not "What If?"

One of the most dangerous questions in our language is "What if?" What if tragedy happens? What if the economy crumbles? What if I or a loved one contract a terrible disease? What if my child goes against the good values we have taught? We can never know "what if" until challenges happen. What we can know is "What IS." We could better express it by saying "Who IS." God is the only hopeful constant in our lives. He told Moses to tell the Israelites, "I AM has sent you." God is not only past tense, "I was with you when..." nor is he only "I will be with you" in a far distant future. He IS what he IS: an ever-present, all-powerful God who is not reduced to a place or time. We can trust that he IS always with each one of us in the midst of every trial and is the source of all hope and joy: past, present and future.

Exodus 3:14,15b
[14] God said to Moses, "I AM WHO I AM. This is what you are to say to the Israelites: 'I AM has sent me to you.'"

[15b]   "This is my name forever,
    the name you shall call me
    from generation to generation."

Matthew 28:18-20
[18] Then Jesus came to them and said, "All authority in heaven and on earth has been given to me. [19] Therefore go and make disciples of all nations, baptizing them in the name of the Father and of the Son and of the Holy Spirit, [20] and teaching them to obey everything I have commanded you. And surely I am with you always, to the very end of the age."

Prayer Guide
Our holy, heavenly Father, may your will prevail. Supply our daily needs. Forgive our sins as we forgive others. Protect us from temptation and rescue us from evil. We pray through the name, power and blood of our Lord, Jesus. Amen.

The Final Focus

On what are we focusing? If every day we reexamine what is wrong, difficult or distressing in life, we will only see trouble. Instead, let us concentrate on our always good Heavenly Father and our Savior, Jesus Christ, who died on the cross that we may be resurrected as he was and live eternally. May we be grateful for the Holy Spirit who guides, comforts and walks beside us continually. We must remember that when all words have been said and all deeds have been done, God's final answer is "Yes!"

John 14:26-27
[26] But the Advocate, the Holy Spirit, whom the Father will send in my name, will teach you all things and will remind you of everything I have said to you. [27] Peace I leave with you; my peace I give you. I do not give to you as the world gives. Do not let your hearts be troubled and do not be afraid.

Revelations 22:20
[20] He who testifies to these things says, "Yes, I am coming soon." Amen. Come, Lord Jesus.

Prayer Guide
Our holy, heavenly Father, may your will prevail. Supply our daily needs. Forgive our sins as we forgive others. Protect us from temptation and rescue us from evil. We pray through the name, power and blood of our Lord, Jesus. Amen.

Pain Is Pain

Whether caused by a knife
Or the words of a "friend"

The loss of a life
Or marriage at an end...
The blows are as bad
Though inside my mind
As sharp and as cutting
As any other kind!

Your pain and my pain
Leave two different marks
And it little matters
Which fires from which sparks.

Whether inside or outside,
The question is this:
Not whose pain is worse,
But how to exist!

So when we can't change the pain
And we simply endure
We must lean on Christ,
Only His love
Is sure.

M. Meinert, 1988

Acknowledgments

I wish to thank my husband, Philip, for his countless hours helping prepare this book of devotions, which has been in my heart and in handwritten notebooks for a period of years. His efforts made it possible. I also greatly appreciate the work of our editor, Edie Edmondson, who taught us what we didn't even know we needed and corrected our many errors. We appreciate Dianna Merrell, graphic designer of Mangy Cat Creative Services, for refining my ideas for the cover design and getting the entire book print ready. MeLissa Houdmann gave us valuable advice, including recommending a qualified editor and skilled graphic designer, as well as "how to proceed" steps along the way due to her extensive editing and writing experience.

Thanks are due to many friends who prayed for a very long time for me to write and print this book, since so many do struggle and need to know that the Bible indeed has the answers because God loves and cares for each one of us.

++++++++++++++
M.Meinert
Creations
LLC
++++++++++++++

Made in the USA
Middletown, DE
29 October 2022